Constitutional Law in Romania

Constitutional Law in Romania

Fourth Edition

Irina Moroianu Zlătescu

This book was originally published as a monograph in the International Encyclopaedia of Laws/Constitutional Law.

Founding Editor: Roger Blanpain†
General Editor: Frank Hendrickx
Volume Editors: André Alen & David Haljan

Wolters Kluwer

Published by:
Kluwer Law International B.V.
PO Box 316
2400 AH Alphen aan den Rijn
The Netherlands
E-mail: lrs-sales@wolterskluwer.com
Website: www.wolterskluwer.com/en/solutions/kluwerlawinternational

Sold and distributed by:
Wolters Kluwer Legal & Regulatory U.S.
920 Links Avenue
Landisville, PA 17538
United States of America
Email: customer.service@wolterskluwer.com

ISBN 978-94-035-6870-6

e-Book: ISBN 978-94-035-6880-5
web-PDF: ISBN 978-94-035-6890-4

The Author

Irina Moroianu Zlătescu, Ph.D., Honoris Causa Doctor, is a Professor of European Law, International Human Rights Law and International Jurisdictions; she holds a doctor's degree and is a postdoctor's degree advisor at the National University for Political Studies and Public Administration (SNSPA), as well as a Professor of Comparative Law and European Law with the Ecological University of Bucharest. She is a titular member of the International Academy of Comparative Law (IACL), the Hague, and also a titular member of the Academy of Legal Sciences of Romania. Professor Zlătescu is Vice President of the International Institute of Law of French Expression and Inspiration (IDEF) and Assessor and MCC of the European Law Institute, a member of the Scientific Board of the International Encyclopaedia of Laws. She is a member of the International Association of Constitutional Law and a member of the French Society of Comparative Legislation. She also carried out activities as a member of the Management Board of the European Union Agency for Fundamental Rights (FRA; 2013–2018) and is also a member of the United Nations Working Group of Experts on People of African Descent (UNWGEPAD) (2002–2011), coordinator of the United Nations Educational, Scientific and Cultural Organization (UNESCO) Chair of Human Rights, Democracy, Peace and Tolerance (1998–2016). She was a member of the Superior Council of Magistracy (2005–2011), Dean and Vice Dean with the National University for Political Studies and Public Administration (1999–2005), and also Professor and Senate member at the Diplomatic Academy (1999–2005). Moreover, she was a founding Director of the Romanian Institute for Human Rights (IRDO/RIHR; 1991–2016). She was a founding member of the Romanian Society of Comparative Law and its Secretary since 1987, a member of the Executive Committee of UNICEF-Romania (1990–1998), she is President of the Romanian Association for the United Nations (ANUROM), also Director of the Transdisciplinary Center for Human Rights (SNSPA). She was National Rapporteur or Co-rapporteur to the International Congresses of IACL of Teheran, Budapest, Caracas, Sidney, Montreal, Athens, Bristol, Brisbane, Utrecht, Washington, Vienna, and Asuncion, also, Rapporteur to the First Intermediate Congress of the IACL of Mexico, the Second Intermediate Congress of the IACL of Taiwan and the Third Intermediate Congress of the IACL of Uruguay, as well as the Centennial and 5th Thematic at the Paris 1 Pantheon, Sorbonne University. A member of the

The Author

International Federation of Journalists, she is the author of many volumes and other works devoted to comparative private and public law, European institutional and substantial law, constitutional law and international human rights law.

Table of Contents

List of Abbreviations

ANUROM	Romanian Association for the United Nations
CFREU	Charter of Fundamental Rights of the European Union
ECHR	European Convention on Human Rights
ECHR-P1	First Optional Protocol to the European Convention on Human Rights
ESCR	European Social Charter Revised
EU	European Union
FRA	European Union Agency for Fundamental Rights
FSN	National Salvation Front
GEO	Government Emergency Ordinance
IACL	International Academy of Comparative Law
NATO	North Atlantic Treaty Organization
RIHR/IRDO	Romanian Institute for Human Rights
UDMR	Uniunea Democratică a Maghiarilor din Romania
UN	United Nations
UNESCO	United Nations Educational, Scientific and Cultural Organization
UNO	United Nations Organization
UNWGEPAD	United Nations Working Group of Experts on People of African Descent

General Introduction

§1. Brief Presentation of the Romanian Constitutional Tradition

1. The foundation of the Romanian Modern State was laid at the beginning of the seventeenth century when the three Romanian Principalities – Muntenia (Walachia), Moldavia and Transylvania – were united for the first time in 1600 by the great Prince Mihai Viteazul (Michael the Brave).

The first document that could be highlighted is 'The Establishment of Constantine Mavrocordat', adopted by the Assemblies of Guilds on 7 February 1741.[1] Mavrocordat used the document to convey to his son advice on governing the country. It embodied a genuine programme of reforms in the fiscal, administrative, agricultural and legal areas. Such a reform programme was later adopted by Alexandru Ioan Cuza in 1864.

During the eighteenth century, the Supplex Libellus Valachorum,[2] adopted in 1791, represented an important political document for the Romanian people in Transylvania, as it embodied the fight for national freedom and expressed the claims of the Romanian people, up to the 1892 Memorandum.

In 1822, a draft constitution was prepared, the so-called Cărvunari Constitution (a name inspired by the Italian term 'carbonaro'), fostering the first germs of democratic traditions in the Romanian principalities. The document included principles of organization and functioning of the state as those adopted by the modern states of the time, inspired by the principles of the French Revolution. These principles were: respect for property and the possibility of expropriation for public use, but with just and prior compensation, individual freedom for which rules and principles were established, freedom of labour and trade, guaranteeing individual honour, and equality before the law. These principles were later taken over into other constitutions.

1. The Establishment (Marele Hrisov) stipulated reforms for Muntenia (Wallachia) and it was published in Mercure de France in 1742. In September 1741, the Prince Mavrocordat, after being sent to the Principality of Moldova, tries to apply the above mentioned Establishment here. *See also* Ioan Ceterchi, (coord), *Istoria dreptului românesc*, vol.2, partea I, Ed. Academiei, Bucureşti, 1984, pp. 23-24; *See* Irina Moroianu Zlătescu, *Constitutional Law in Romania* (2nd ed., Wolters Kluwer International BV, 2017) pp. 11ff.
2. David Prodan, *Supplex Libellus Valachorum: din istoria fomării naţiunii române* (Editura Enciclopedică, Bucureşti, 2013), p. 74.

We should like to mention also the adoption of Organic Regulations by Wallachia (1831) and Moldova (1832)[3] as an important moment, as well as the Statute which expands the Paris Convention. Even though there were some other drafts, for example, the Draft Constitution drawn up by Ion Câmpineanu in 1838,[4] or the one drawn up by Mihail Kogălniceanu in 1848, for twenty-seven years, these documents had been a substitute Constitution in the Romanian principalities; many of their provisions remained in force until 1864, and some of them even longer, after 1900.

Another document worth mentioning is the Proclamation of Islaz (8–9 June 1848) which, *inter alia*, required for the first time the establishment of the 'Republic' as a form of government. It became the only Romanian source[5] of the Constitution Mihail Kogălniceanu drafted during the same year, a document that was 'legally and politically influenced by the foreign democratic Constitutions'.[6]

The union of the Romanian Principalities proved ephemeral: Transylvania gradually fell under the domination of the Habsburg Empire, while Walachia and Moldavia were successively dominated by the Ottoman Empire and the Tsarist one.

However, the unionist ideal had been kept alive in the hearts of the populations of the three principalities and, in 1859, it was partly achieved by the unification of Moldavia and Walachia. The new State was at first called the 'United Principalities' and later 'Romania'. Prince Alexandru Ioan Cuza (1859–1866) played an important role in the modern organization of the Romanian State. In 1877, as a result of the Russian-Romanian-Turkish war, Romania, led by Prince Charles I of Hohenzollern-Sigmaringen, proclaimed its independence (till then it had been dominated by the Ottoman Empire, with a strong autonomy). The independence, however, was to be acknowledged only four years later, in 1881. That same year, Prince Charles I was crowned King of Romania and the country became the Kingdom of Romania. It was to remain so till after World War II when, in 1947, the communist regime forced King Michael I to abdicate.

The national unity of the entire Romanian people was achieved after the victory obtained in World War I, where Romania was allied to the Triple Entente. Thus, on 27 March 1918, Bessarabia (the eastern part of Moldavia), which had proclaimed its independence from Soviet Russia under the name of the Democratic Republic of Moldavia, united with Romania. It was followed by Bucovina, a former province of the Habsburg Empire, which united with Romania on 15 November 1918.

Finally, Transylvania, together with Crişana, Maramureş and Banat, united with Romania as a result of a decision by the Great National Assembly in Alba Iulia, on 18 November 1918.

3. Irina Moroianu Zlătescu, *Human Rights: A Dynamic and Evolving Process* (Editura Pro Universitaria, Bucureşti, 2025), pp. 53–54.
4. This draft stated the idea of reaching national independence and some human rights and liberties, such as equality before the law, personal freedom, freedom of speech, freedom of the press, and so on. *See* Alexandru Lapedatu, *Ion Câmpineanu (1798–1863)* (Editura Cartea Românească, Bucureşti, 1937), p. 18.
5. Dionisie Ionescu and Gheorghe Ţuţui, Gheorghe Matei, *Dezvoltarea constituţională a statului român* (Editura Ştiinţifică Bucureşti, 1957), p. 108.
6. Alexandru Tilman-Timon, *Les influences etrangères sur le droit constitutionnel roumain* (Sirey, Paris, 1946), p. 280.

In 1940, after the Molotov-Ribbentrop Agreement had been concluded, Soviet Russia occupied, following an ultimatum, Bessarabia and Northern Bucovina (a province that had never been a Russian possession). The same year, by the Dictate of Vienna imposed by Hitler and Mussolini, Northern Transylvania was surrendered to Hungary. Also in 1940, the southern part of Dobrogea, called the Quadrilateral, was surrendered to Bulgaria.

It was only after the victory of the Allies in World War II that the occupied territory of Transylvania came back to Romania. However, the other territories lost by Romania during World War II (Bessarabia, Northern Bucovina and the Quadrilateral) have never been recovered.

On 6 March 1945, Romania, which had already fallen into the zone of Soviet influence, was imposed a communist government by means of massive electoral fraud, while on 30 December 1947, the king was compelled to abdicate and the Popular Republic of Romania was instituted. The communist regime was abolished on 22 December 1989, as a result of the Romanian Revolution. In 1991, a new Constitution[7] was adopted, which reaffirmed the democratic values shown within the 1866 and 1923 Constitutions, and adapted them to the new political realities of the time. Soon after, Romania became a member of the Council of Europe, and we should also mention that it ratified the most important document of this organization, more specifically the European Convention on Human Rights (ECHR) and Fundamental Freedoms.[8] Later on, in 2003, the fundamental law was revised,[9] especially in view of Romania's accession to the North Atlantic Treaty Organization (NATO) and the European Union (EU).

2. Except for the two organic regulations – acts of a constitutional nature – promulgated in the Danube Principalities – Moldavia and Walachia – in 1830 under Russian domination, the first constitutional act of the United Principalities may be considered to have been the Developing Statute of the Convention of 7/19 August 1858 of the United Principalities.

This Convention, concluded in Paris after the Crimean War between the Ottoman Empire and the Guaranteeing Powers, guaranteed the autonomy of the United Principalities.

Prior to gaining full independence from Ottoman power, the Statute proclaimed that the Convention should remain Romania's fundamental law. It conferred on the United Principalities a very broad autonomy in all fields of activity.

The Statute provided that public powers were entrusted to the ruler (Prince), a pondering assembly (kind of present-day Senate) and an elective assembly (kind of

7. Adopted within the meeting of the Constituent Assembly on 21 Nov. 1991, published in the Monitorul Oficial, Part I, No. 233/21.11.1991, coming into force after its approval by the national referendum of 8 Dec. 1991.
8. By Law No. 30/18.5.1994, published in the Monitorul Oficial, Part I, No. 135/31.5.1994 (according to the Decision No. 146/14.7.2000 of the Constitutional Court of Romania, published in the Monitorul Oficial, Part I, No. 566/15.10.2000, the ratification of this Convention by Romania implied that the Convention was adopted within the national legal system, and referring to it received the same force as referring to the Constitution).
9. *See* Law No. 429/23.10.2003, published in the Monitorul Oficial, Part I, No. 758/28.10.2003.

present-day Chamber of Deputies). The legislative power was to be exercised collectively by the ruler and the two assemblies, but it was only the ruler that had the right to legislative initiative.

The Statute was accompanied by an Electoral Act. Both were adopted after they had been subjected to a referendum by Prince Alexandru Ioan Cuza.

3. Romania's first proper Constitution was issued in 1866[10] and was adopted after independence had been gained. It was further subject to a number of amendments, particularly after proclamation of the Kingdom, when it became the Constitution of the Kingdom of Romania.

Elaborated after the model of the Belgian Constitution, it provided, among others, that the Kingdom of Romania, together with its counties on the right bank of the Danube, constituted an indivisible State.

The Constitution provided for a large number of citizens' rights, which gave it a widely democratic nature.

For instance, Article 7 proclaimed that differences in religious faith and confession should not constitute a barrier against access to the civil and political rights and the exercise thereof. It also proclaimed that the State should make no discrimination as to social class and that all citizens were equal before the law and had the duty to make their contribution to the public treasury and tasks.

4. The Constitution guaranteed, among other things:

1. individual freedom and inviolability of the domicile;
2. protection of aliens residing on the territory of Romania, equal to the protection provided by the law to autochthonous persons and property;
3. respect of the principle of the legality of incrimination and sanctioning (*nullum crimen sine lege*; *nulla poena sine lege*);
4. the sacred and inviolable nature of property of any kind, as well as the State treasury;
5. that expropriation could only be made for reasons of public utility, legally attested, and only after fair and previous redress;
6. freedom of conscience and freedom of religion (Article 21) to the extent practice thereof did not infringe upon public order or good morals;[11]
7. freedom of education to the extent it did not infringe upon public order and good morals;[12] and
8. freedom of communication and the freedom to publish ideas and opinions.

10. This Constitution was revised on 12 Oct. 1879, on 8 Jun. 1884 and on 19 Jul. 1917. *See* Irina Moroianu Zlătescu, *Dreptul drepturilor omului, Editura Universitară* (Editura Universul Academic, Bucureşti, 2025), pp. 87–88.
11. The Orthodox Religion of the East was proclaimed 'the dominant religion of the Romanian State'. The Romanian Orthodox Church was independent of any foreign hierarchy, while it kept its dogmatic unity with the Ecumenical Church of the East.
12. Education in the state-owned schools was free of charge, while primary education was compulsory.

The Constitution prohibited (the list is not exhaustive):

1. all sorts of privileges, exemptions and monopolies;
2. foreign titles of nobility;
3. the property-confiscation penalty;
4. death penalty, except for the cases provided for by the Military Criminal Code in case of war;
5. the adoption of any restrictive law in terms of communication;
6. censorship and other preventive measures for the issuing or distribution of any publication;
7. the requirement of previous authorization for publication;
8. putting the press under a warning regime; and
9. suspension or suppression of any newspaper or publication.

5. As far as the powers within the State are concerned, the Constitution reflected the theory of the separation of powers. It provided that all powers within the State were the issue in the nation, which could only exercise them by delegation.

The legislative power was exercised collectively by the King and the national representation formed by the Senate and the Deputies' Assembly.

Although it granted legislative initiative to all three branches of the legislative power, the Constitution provided that any law referring to the State's income and expenditures or the military conscription had to be first passed by the Deputies' Assembly.

The executive power was entrusted to the King, who exercised it as provided for by the Constitution.

The exclusive interests of the counties or of the communes were entrusted to the Local Councils.

As regards the national representation, the electorate in each county was divided into three colleges according to the incomes of the electors, which were established in different ways.

The King's constitutional powers were hereditary – it was the first time that a Romanian Constitution was so provided – while the Salic law, privileging the masculine offspring, with continuous exclusion of women and their descendants, was applied.

6. Only a Romanian person or a naturalized Romanian was eligible to be a minister. The members of the royal family were also excluded from this office.

The ministers, who were not members of the Assemblies, were permitted to participate in the debates on the laws, but they had no right to vote in the end.

As regards the army, the Constitution provided that every citizen was part of the 'elements of the armed forces, according to the special laws', while the enrolment of the army was voted every year.

7. The national unity of all Romanian provinces was achieved in 1918, when the completion of the Romanian territory was reached, as a result of the union of Transylvania, Bessarabia and Bukovina with the Country,[13] so a new Fundamental Act was needed. The Constitution of 28 March 1923[14] was the first Constitution of reunited Romania. Moreover, this fundamental act represents the first democratic Constitution of the country.[15] It took over a great number of texts from the one that had preceded it. Modifications as compared to the previous Constitution were not numerous.

Its first article states that the Kingdom of Romania was a national, unitary and indivisible State and that its territory was inalienable.

Most important was the text that provided for the 'rights of Romanians'.[16] It brought together such a wide range of rights and freedoms that the Constitution of 1923 was considered the most liberal constitution.

All citizens, irrespective of ethnic origin, mother tongue or religious faith, were granted a large series of freedoms: freedom of thought, education, the press, assembly, association, and 'all freedoms and rights established by the law' (Article 5).

According to the Constitution, women's civil rights were to be established on the basis of full equality between the two sexes. Regarding the conditions that had to be met for women to be able to exercise their political rights, the Constitution provided that they were to be established by special laws voted by a two-thirds majority.

The constitutional text also provided that differences of religious faith and confession or of ethnic origin would not constitute a barrier against access to civil and political rights and the exercise thereof.

It was ruled that foreigners could be granted the political rights enjoyed by Romanians only through naturalization.

Individual freedom was guaranteed, as were the rights of a person in case of search, detention or arrest. Also, the principle of the legality of incrimination and penalty was enshrined, while the property-confiscation penalty and, in times of peace, the death penalty were prohibited.

Property of any kind was guaranteed and so were the State's debts. However, only Romanians and those naturalized as Romanians could obtain rural houses in Romania, while foreigners were only entitled to the value of these houses.

---

13. We must mention the Alba-Iulia Declaration, by which it was decided, on 1 Dec. 1918, the unification of Transylvania, Banat, Criana and Maramureş with the Romanian Kingdom.
14. The 1923 Constitution repeals also the 1866 Constitution and its subsequent amendments, except for Law Nos 3092/1918, 2085/1919 and 3464/1919, which had implicitly modified the previous Constitution and which are ratified by the new Constitution.
15. The Constitution of 1923 assumed most of the provisions of the Constitution of 1866, having ten articles in addition; some of the articles of the old Constitution were amended, and a few have received a new content.
16. In this regard, *see* Adrian Năstase, *Drepturile omului: Religie a sfârşitului de secol* (Editura IRDO, Bucureşti, 1992), p. 118; Ioan Alexandru, *100 de ani in evoluţia dreptului administrativ din România*, in *Evolutia dreptului si a societăţii româneşti în context internaţional 1918–2018* (Editura Universitară, Editura Universul Academic, Bucureşti, 2019), p. 14.

8. The Constitution consecrated the principle of separation of powers. The legislative power was exercised by the King and the national representation formed by the Senate and the Deputies' Assembly, while laws could only be adopted through participation of these three actors.

The King had the executive power. Succession to the throne followed the Salic law tradition, which gave prevalence to the male branch with continuous exclusion of women and their descendants.

A new provision referred to the courts of law, continuing the praetorian practice preceding the Court of Cassation, according to which it was only the latter that had the right to rule, in joint sessions, on the constitutionality of laws and to declare as inapplicable those laws that conflicted with the Constitution. It is worth mentioning that it provided that administrative disputes fell under the competence of the judiciary and that no special authorities could be established for the settlement of administrative disputes.

9. The next Constitution of Romania was passed in 1938.[17] It was adopted under the authoritarian reign of King Charles II after a referendum and applied only for two years, between 27 February 1938 and 5 September 1940, when it was suspended by a Royal Decree.

The constitutional text was organized into eight titles and 100 articles. In comparison to the preceding constitution, this one was less undemocratic for several reasons, including the fact that the universal suffrage had been removed and the king was proclaimed head of the State in which capacity he exercised all political powers himself, being the only entity through which the nation could exercise its powers.

While, as far as the citizens' rights and duties were concerned, the new Constitution did not deviate too much from the one that had preceded it, an interesting point was contained in Title III, entitled 'On the State's Powers'.

Though all powers within the State emanated from the Romanian Nation (Article 29), it was the King who exercised the legislative power through the National Representation composed of the Senate and the National Assembly. The King sanctioned and promulgated the laws. Prior to being sanctioned, a law was not effective. The King could refuse to sanction a law.

The undemocratic nature of the Constitution of 1938 also came from the fact that it conferred extremely large powers to the King. This included, among many others, the prerogative to make regulations needed for the execution of laws, without being able, however, to modify them or exempt anyone from execution thereof. He also had the power to issue decrees with the power of law when the legislative assemblies were dissolved or during their inter-session interval; these decrees were to be submitted to the assemblies for ratification in the next session. The King also had the prerogative to appoint or confirm persons in public offices and could declare war or make peace. He also had the right to coin money.

---

17. Published in the Monitorul Oficial, Part I, No. 48, on 27 Feb. 1938. *See also* Andreea Stănciulescu (Alexe), *Puterea constituantă*. Teoria şi practica puterii constituante (Editura C.H.Beck, Bucureşti, 2019), pp. 181 and the following.

On 5 September 1940, the Constitution was suspended by Royal Decree. Romania joined the war in June 1941 in alliance with the Axis powers, and left this alliance on 23 August 1944, continuing the war alongside the Allies. Given this context, the Constitution was made partially effective again on 2 September 1944,[18] and it was modified shortly after, in October, the same year.[19] It was amended in 1946 specifically regarding the exercise of the legislative power.[20] It was expressly abolished on 30 December 1947 by Law No. 363/30.12.1947,[21] when the King was dethroned.

10. A new Constitution, the first Constitution of the communist regime, was adopted on 13 April 1948,[22] as it abolished the monarchy while proclaiming the Romanian People's Republic.

This new Constitution started from the idea of the unity of power. Totalitarianism primarily means rejection of the separation of powers theory and concentration of power in a single hand. It is this meaning that has to be given to the provisions of Article 3: 'In the Romanian People's Republic, the entire power emanates from the people and belongs to the people.' A striking difference in comparison to all previous constitutions was the way this Constitution regulated property. Of course, in 1948, State property was poorly developed. Nationalization of the main means of production was only achieved on 11 June 1948, on the basis of the Constitution. The latter created the premise of a 'unique fund of State property'. It proclaimed that 'the means of production belonged to the State, as assets of the entire people or of the cooperative organizations or of private persons, natural or legal'. It was also proclaimed that any assets in the subsoil, ore deposits, forests, waters, natural energy sources, railways, roads, water and air navigation ways, the post, the telegraph, the telephone and the radio belonged to the State, as common assets of the people.

The Constitution proclaimed that 'The people's common assets constitute the material basis for the economic welfare and national independence of the Romanian People's Republic' (Article 7), while according to Article 11, 'when the general interest demands it, the means of production, the banks and the insurance companies, that are the private property of natural or legal persons, may become property of the State, that is, the people's asset, under the conditions provided for by the law'. Also, domestic and foreign trade was regulated and controlled by the State and exercised by state-owned, private and cooperative trade companies, while planning the national economy became one of the Government's main tasks.

---

18. By Royal Decree No. 1626/31.8.1944 on establishing the rights of the Romanians within the frame of the 1866 Constitution, and within the amendments of the Constitution adopted on 29 Mar. 1923, signed by King Mihai I, and published in the Monitorul Oficial No. 202/2.9.1944.
19. The Royal Decree No. 1626/1944 was amended by Royal Decree No. 1849/1944 published in the Monitorul Oficial No. 235/11.10.1944. Given this, the 1923 Constitution was also modified.
20. By Royal Decree No. 2218/1946, published in the Monitorul Oficial No. 161/15.7.1946. In the same Monitorul Oficial, Law No. 560/15.7.1946 was published, in reference to the election of the Deputies Chamber. This law was enacted by Royal Decree 2219/1946.
21. Law No. 363/30.12.1947 on the establishment of the Romanian State as the Romanian People's Republic, enacted by Decree No. 2299/30.12.1947, published in the Monitorul Oficial No. 300 *bis*/30.12.1947.
22. Published in the Monitorul Oficial, Part I, No. 87 *bis*/13.4.1948.

11. The Constitution established popular councils as local bodies of State authority. They were led by executive committees which represented their managing and executive bodies. Owing to the principle of the uniqueness of power, the popular councils (qualified as bodies of local authority), as well as their executive committees, were subordinated both to the higher popular councils and executive committees, also, at the same time, to the State-central administration bodies.

12. As far as the judicial hierarchy is concerned, the Supreme Court was the Pyramid Peak. The courts, with the exception of the Supreme Court, ruled on cases with the participation of popular assessors.

Article 96 provided that the public prosecutor's main task was to pursue and punish crimes 'against the democratic order and freedom, the economic interests, the independence and sovereignty of the Romanian State', a text that enabled it to play a major role in the repression of any anti-communist activity.

13. The second communist Constitution was adopted by the Great National Assembly on 24 September 1952,[23] after a period when the totalitarian regime had been considerably consolidated and the national economy had been subjected to central planning. According to the Constitution, the Romanian People's Republic is a State of the working people living in towns and villages.

The basis of the popular power is the alliance between the working class and the working peasantry, while the leading role belongs to the working class. The Romanian People's Republic was born and strengthened (Article 3) 'as a result of the country's liberation by the armed forces of the Soviet Union from the fascist yoke and imperialist domination, as a result of the overthrowing of landowners and capitalists by the popular masses in towns and villages led by the working class, under the leadership of the Romanian Communist Party'.

Article 4 provided that the power belonged to the working people in towns and villages, who exercised it through the Great National Assembly and the Popular Councils, which represented the 'political basis of the Republic'.

The economy included three sectors: the socialist one, the small production of goods, and the private-capitalist sector.

The basis of the socialist sector was the common ownership of the means of production, either as State property (qualified as the people's common asset) or as cooperative-collectivist property (agricultural collective farms or cooperative organizations).

According to the Constitution, all assets of the subsoil, the factories, the plants and the mines, the forests, the waters, the natural energy sources, all communication ways, railway transportation, river, sea and air transportation, the banks, the post, the telegraph, the telephone, the radio, the printing devices, the cinema and the theatre, the state-owned agricultural farms, the machines and tractor stations, the communal enterprises, as well as the nationalized part of the housing in towns, constituted a common asset of the people.

However, the land belonged to those who toiled on it and was not, in principle, State property (Article 8).

---

23. It was published in the Monitorul Oficial, Part I, No. 1/27.9.1952.

14. As far as the system of State bodies was concerned, the new Constitution changed close to nothing as compared to the preceding one: the Great National Assembly remained the unique legislating body. Its Presidium enjoyed, at the same time, the powers of the Presidency of the State. However, a new element was that after stating that 'the supreme executive and command body of the State power' was the Council of Ministers, which was 'constituted by the Great National Assembly', it listed all the offices of ministers and presidents of State committees that were included in it and also specified the names of the ministries.

15. The new Constitution recognized the same rights and freedoms as its predecessor. It is worth mentioning that the right to strike was not recognized. Even though Stalin died in 1953, political repression continued.

The Constitution of 1952 was effective until 21 August 1965, when the Constitution of the Socialist Republic of Romania was adopted. While proclaiming that the State was a 'Socialist Republic', the new Constitution laid down that the leading political force of the entire society was the Romanian Communist Party. It was also provided that Romania's national economy was a socialist economy, based upon socialist ownership of the means of production.

The Constitution of 1965[24] introduced a new administrative-territorial organization. Thus, instead of regions and districts, another category of units emerged: the county, the town, and the commune. The most important towns could be organized as municipalities, while the municipality of Bucharest was organized into sectors.

The citizens' rights and duties were given an ample chapter, including the right of a person whose rights had been infringed by an illegal act of a State body to apply to the competent bodies for annulment of the act and redress. A subsequent law established that the ruling of cases fell under the competence of courts of law. However, it was hardly applied because of the very small and insignificant number of acts that could be attacked and because the courts admitted such actions quite seldom.

In comparison to the previous communist constitutions, the provisions related to the State bodies were subject to modifications. While the Great National Assembly remained the supreme body of power and the unique legislative body, the Presidium, however, was replaced by the State Council – defined as 'the supreme body with permanent activity, subordinated to the Great National Assembly'.

The sessions of the Great National Assembly were few in number and usually had propagandistic purposes. Between sessions, the State Council could promulgate

24. Published in the Monitorul Oficial, Part I, No. 1/21.8.1965. It was modified by Law No. 1/1968, published in the Monitorul Oficial, Part I, No. 16.2.1968; Law No. 56/1968, published in the Monitorul Oficial, Part I, No. 168/26.12.1968; Law No. 1/1969, published in the Monitorul Oficial, Part I, No. 31/13.3.1969; Law No. 26/1971, published in the Monitorul Oficial, Part I, No. 157/17.12.1971; Law No. 1/1972, published in the Monitorul Oficial, Part I, No. 41/24.4.1972; Law No. 1/1974, published in the Monitorul Oficial, Part I, No. 45/28.3.1974; Law No. 66/1974, published in the Monitorul Oficial, Part I, No. 161/23.12.1974; Law No. 2/1975, published in the Monitorul Oficial, Part I, No. 30/21.3.1975; Law No. 19/1979, published in the Monitorul Oficial, Part I, No. 103/19.12.1979; Law No. 19/1986, published in the Monitorul Oficial, Part I, No. 64/27.10.1986.

norms with the power of law, with the exception of amendments to the Constitution. According to the procedure for the adoption of laws, these were submitted to the Great National Assembly convened in its next session.

Also, a new element was the establishment of the office of President of the Republic by the modification of the Constitution that took place in 1974. The President was qualified as the Head of State, who represented the State's power in domestic and international relations. He was, at the same time, the supreme commander of the armed forces and the President of the Council of National Defence. He also presided over the State Council.

16. By the year 1989, the living standard of the Romanian people had dramatically worsened. The 'magnificent' socialist economy was on the verge of bankruptcy. Lack of political and civil rights had for some time now been added to lack of basic aliments (bread, flour, sugar, milk, meat, oil, etc.), energy (electricity, heating, fuel), hot and cold water, etc., everything on a general background of increased communist propaganda and increased cult of personality.

Under the circumstances, it came as no surprise that a tiny spark (the abusive arrest of a minister in Timişoara) lit the fire of massive revolt, which eventually turned into genuine revolution. The date of 22 December 1989 marked the victory of the Romanian Revolution and the collapse of the communist regime. The new democratic regime proclaimed the elimination of the communist State's structures. The old Constitution had not yet been formally abrogated, but the only part that remained applicable was the one referring to the citizens' rights and duties.

The period between the fall of the communism and the adoption of the new Constitution had, according to a part of the doctrine, two stages:[25] the stage of the revolutionary power and the stage of the legalisation of the revolution. According to other authors, there were four stages: the establishment of a real, de facto, government; the adoption of Law No. 31/1990 on the Temporary Council of National Union; the adoption of Law No. 92/1990 regarding the election of the Parliament and of the president; the adoption of the Constitution.[26] Historically, one should mention that: on 22 December 1989, the National Salvation Front (FSN) was created and the Council of the FSN, within the Front, got the entire power, that *'proposed that the country to be named from now on Romania'*.[27] Under these historical conditions, the Council was given the exercise of state power, and the Communiqué issued on the same day announced the forming of a Committee for drafting the Constitution, which was effective immediately. This implied some

25. *See* Tudor Drăganu, *Drept constituţional şi instituţii politice*. Tratat elementar, vol.1, Bucureşti, Editura Lumina Lex, 1998, pp. 390-407; *See also* Cristian Ionescu, *Tratat de drept constituţional contemporan,* ed. 3, Bucureşti: Editura C.H. Beck, 2019, pp. 613-620; Marius Bălan, *Drept constituţional şi instituţii politice, vol.1, Teoria Generală a statului şi a constituţiei. Constituţia română în context contemporan*, Bucureşti, Ed. Hamangiu, 2015, pp. 271-281.

26. Ion Deleanu, *Instituţii şi proceduri constituţionale: în dreptul român şi în dreptul comparat,* Bucureşti: Editura C.H. Beck, 2006.

27. The Communiqué of the FSN published in the Monitorul Oficial, No. 1/22.12.1989.

preliminary measures, for example, opening the door for new political parties, thus reinstating the multi-party system and democracy in Romania.[28]

On 31 December 1989, Decree-Law No. 8 was adopted. It regulated the registration and functioning of political parties and public organizations, reinstated political pluralism in Romania and enshrined the freedom to establish political parties while also prohibiting the establishment of fascist parties or parties propagating concepts jeopardizing the legal order and the rule of law. Decree-Law No. 8 also established the purposes of the political parties, which had to be in consonance with the legal order and the rule of law in Romania and promote respect for the sovereignty, independence and national integrity of Romania, democracy, the citizens' freedoms and rights and assert the dignity of the Romanian nation. Persons who were incompatible with the quality of party members included diplomats, magistrates, the staff of the Ministry of National Defence, the staff of the Ministry of Internal Affairs, and the operative staff of the public radio and television companies.

On 9 February 1990, Decree-Law No. 81/1990 was adopted. It included provisions referring to the Provisional National Unity Council, and turned the FSN into a political party; the Council of the FSN was replaced by the Provisional National Unity Council, the latter being made up based on the principle of parity as a parliament that adopted decree-laws.

Decree-Law No. 92/1990[29] was adopted on 14 March 1990. It concerned the election of Parliament and of the President of Romania, establishing an important number of constitutional norms, which were to be applied for a limited period of time, till the adoption of a new Constitution. The regulations of this Decree-Law regarded more than the organization of the new elections, meaning it also stipulated a series of principles on the relations between the President, the Parliament and the Government, as well as principles concerning the competence and the manner of electing the Assembly of Deputies, the Senate and the President, and also some new principles of governance.

Also, a constituent assembly was elected. It had the function of an ordinary Parliament as well and on 21 November 1991, it passed the new Constitution, which was the expression of the initial constituant body.[30] This Constitution was subjected, on 8 December 1991, to a national referendum which approved it with 77.31% of the expressed votes. The Constitution became effective on the date of its approval by referendum.

There have been some initiatives concerning the revision of the Constitution. We would like to mention that, according tot he doctrine, following the actual revision procedure, as stated in the Constitution, represent an external constitutional control mechanism, and abiding by the material limits regarding revision represent internal control mechanism.[31] Thus, let us name the initiative of the Parliament, in 1996, regarding Article 41(7) of the Constitution of 1991, related to the presumption of

28. Decree-Law No. 8/31.12.1989 on Registering and Functioning of Political Parties and Public Organizations in Romania.
29. Published in the Monitorul Oficial, No. 35/18.3.1990.
30. *See* Dan Claudiu Dănişor, *Putere şi autoritate constituantă în România revoluţionară*, în Pandectele Române, nr.1/2018, pp. 91-105.
31. Toader Tudorel, Marieta Safta, Curs de contencios constituţional, Bucureşti, Editura Hamangiu, 2017, pp. 100-105.

lawful acquisition of wealth,[32] and the citizens' initiative in 2000, regarding the provisions of Article 41(2) related to the right to private property.[33]

As will be shown further, the Constitution was revised under the Constitutional Act No. 429/2003.[34] The Constitutional Act was approved by the referendum of 18–19 October 2003, whose results were confirmed by the Constitutional Court under Decision No. 3 of 22 October 2003.

32. *See* the Decision of the Constitutional Court No. 85/3.9.1996, published in the Monitorul Oficial, Part I, No. 211/6.9.1996.
33. *See* the Decision of the Constitutional Court No. 82/27.4.2000, published in the Monitorul Oficial, Part I, No. 193/4.5.2000.
34. Published in the Monitorul Oficial, Part I, No. 758/29.10.2003, approved by national referendum, came into force on 29 Oct. 2003. It was republished and renumbered by the Legislative Council, following the update of some terms, in the Monitorul Oficial, Part I, No. 767/31.10.2003.

Part I. The Constitution of 1991, Revised in 2003: The Beginning of a New Era

17. Constitutions are adopted at a certain moment, but they are meant for the future; so, they represent both a reflection of the time of adoption and a programme for history.[35]

A constitution is the result of specific historical, political, social and economic conditions. Its importance for the democratic functioning of the State's institutions and the society is essential, since it is the Constitution that regulates both the citizens' fundamental rights and the principles for the organization and function of powers within a State. It is for this particular reason that the modern constitutional law has imposed the principle of constitutional stability, according to which the modification of a State's fundamental law should occur after long periods of time, depending on the transformations taking place in society, on their periodicity and on their intensiveness. Nevertheless, the need for revising the Constitution may arise earlier than the doctrine would be willing to accept, and this is so for objective imperatives that go beyond the theoretical estimations. This was the case, for instance, with the Constitution of France adopted in 1958, which only ten years later had to be fundamentally modified in terms of the election of the President of the Republic. A similar situation, characterized by the historic imperatives of Romania's accession to NATO[36] and the EU,[37] as well as the specific conditions of the transition period, was faced by Romania in the year 2003.

18. The Constitution of a new Romania, free from communism, had been adopted by referendum on 8 December 1991; its role was to consecrate the new political, social and economic order created in Romania as a result of the Revolution of December 1989.[38] It was consonant with the legislating exigencies of the

35. *See* Irina Moroianu Zlătescu, *Constitutional Law in Romania* (Wolters Kluwer Law and Business, 2023), pp. 23 and the following.
36. Accession to NATO was achieved on 29 Mar. 2004. Regarding this topic, *see* Irina Moroianu Zlătescu and Radu C. Demetrescu, *Drept instituţional european* şi politici comunitare (Casa Editorială Calistrat Hogaş, Bucureşti, 2001), pp. 40–41; Adrian Năstase, *România Europeană* (Editura MondoMedia, Bucureşti, 2007), p. 87.
37. Accession to EU was achieved on 1 Jan. 2007. Regarding this topic, *see* Irina Moroianu Zlătescu and Elena Marinică, *Dreptul Uniunii Europene* (Editura Universitară, Editura Universul Academic, Bucureşti, 2017), p. 55; Năstase, *România Europeană, supra*, pp. 87, 153 and the following.
38. *See* Vasile Gionea, et al., *Partidele politice* (Editura Regia Autonomă 'Monitorul Oficial', Bucureşti, 1993), pp. 21 and the following; Tudor Drăganu, *Drept constituţional şi instituţii politice. Tratat elementar* (Editura Lumina Lex, Bucureşti), 2000, pp. 11 and the following; Antonie Iorgovan,

Romanian society at that particular moment, when the authorities so made their choices to also include the possibility of setting up forms and entities that were to have their content clarified at a later moment.

19. As a result of the revision of the Constitution in 2003, a new fundamental right was adopted – the right to environment; and new transitory dispositions were also introduced. Of course, revision of the Constitution during the year 2003, amended by referendum on 18 October 2003, and the new text took effect on 29 October 2003. The purpose was also to eliminate as much as possible the imperfections of the text that had been noticed particularly in practice and, most of all, to allow for Romania's integration in the EU and NATO, and so the total number of articles reached 156, these specified that both could take place by parliamentary vote alone, and that EU citizens living in Romania can vote and run for local elections. The revised Constitution enlarges the guarantees for human rights and the fundamental freedoms[39] and also optimizes the decision-making process at the level of public authorities as well as the organization and functioning of some of them, persons belonging to minorities having the right to use their own language when dealing with local administration and the courts, improving the functioning of the legislative chambers, restricting the parliamentary immunity for political declarations, extending the president's to five years, and by explicitly guaranteeing rather than protecting the right to private property and suspending the constitutional obligation for conscription in 2007 until the end of 2025. By Law No. 5/9.1.2026,[40] supplementing Law No. 446/2006 (published in Monitorul Oficial Partea I/No. 990/ 12.12 2006), on population defense strategy, a voluntary conscription procedure was established, for individuals (both men and women), where they can undergo paid military training for a period of four months, while having similar rights to the regular military, in order to increase military human resources in case of military mobilization. Revision of a Constitution, as well as its adoption, is however a delicate exercise of democracy and political negotiation, which involves making the various political forces and currents of thinking come to terms, while interpretation of the juridical solutions, particularly the most difficult ones, has to be achieved by also taking into account such aspects. The ideal with constitutionalism is to achieve a Constitution that gives expression to the 'agreement' reached by the country's political forces after laborious negotiations. This is the reason why the texts of a Constitution or, as the case may be, the texts of a law on the revision of a Constitution, sometimes include solutions reflecting the results of a political compromise. There

---

Tratat de drept administrativ (vol. I, ed. a 4-a. Editura All Beck, 2005), pp. 5 and the following; Ion Deleanu, *Instituţii şi proceduri constituţionale – în dreptul român şi în dreptul comparat* (Editura C.H. Beck, Bucureşti, 2006), pp. 34 and the following; Cristian Ionescu, *Instituţii politice şi drept constituţional* (Editura Juridică, Bucureşti, 2006), pp. 3 and the following; Ion Popescu-Slăniceanu, et al., *Drept administrativ* (Editura Universitară Danubius, Galaţi, 2009), pp. 6 and the following; Gheorghe Iancu, *Drept constituţional şi instituţii politice. Tratat* (Editura C.H. Beck, Bucureşti, 2010), pp. 17 and the following; Dana Tofan, *Drept administrativ* (vol. I, Editura C.H. Beck, Bucureşti, 2020), pp. 4 and the following.

39. *See* Irina Moroianu Zlătescu, *Dreptul Internaţional al Drepturilor Omului* (Editura Universitară, Editura Universul Academic, Bucureşti, 2025), pp. 265 and the following.

40. Published in Monitorul Oficial, Part I, No. 10/9.1.2026.

were also a few reform attempts in the early 2010s, for example, the one after the major political crisis in the second half of 2012. In 2018, a referendum took place regarding Article 48, but it failed, as the turnout was below the required 30%. More detailed analysis shall follow later on.

This is also the reason why the following presentation of the Constitution of Romania refers both to the text of 1991 and the revised and supplemented text of 2003 and includes comments meant to clarify the sources of the constitutional provisions as well as the modifications that were operated, while the analysis is enriched with elements of comparative law and illustrations in the international regulations in the field.

Chapter 1. The Romanian State

20. Article 1 of the Constitution stipulates that Romania is a sovereign, independent, unitary and indivisible National State. The ruling form of the State is the republic. The first two paragraphs of Article 1 remained unchanged in the revised text of 2003. They refer to the characteristic features of the State, which are essential for defining the State in the framework of constitutional democracy. It is in these features that the other characteristic elements are rooted. They are stipulated in paragraph 3 (which was considerably enriched in the text of 2003):[41]

> a democratic and social state, governed by the rule of law,[42] in which human dignity, the citizens' rights and freedoms, the free development of human personality, justice and political pluralism represent supreme values, in the spirit of the democratic traditions of the Romanian people and the ideals of the Revolution of December 1989, and shall be guaranteed.

The revised text of 2003 introduced in Article 1 the phrase 'in the spirit of the democratic traditions of the Romanian people and the ideals of the Revolution of December 1989' and two additional paragraphs 4 and 5, which refer to two fundamental principles: the separation and balance of powers and supremacy of the Constitution and the compulsory nature of the Constitution and the laws.[43]

To illustrate the characteristic features of the country's constitutional system, as reflected in the Constitution of 1991, such as it was revised in 2003, the following issues should be dealt with: the national character of the State; State sovereignty; the unitary and indivisible character of the State; the rule of law principle; the democratic and social character of the State; and constitutional democracy. Prior to approaching these aspects, a few explanations on the republican ruling form are necessary.

---

41. In reference to Art. 1 para. (3), *see* Decision No. 70/18.4.2000 of the Constitutional Court, published in the Monitorul Oficial, Part I, No. 334/19.7.2000, *see also* Decision No. 17/21.1.2015 of the Constitutional Court, published in the Monitorul Oficial, Part I, No. 79/30.1.2015.
42. Regarding the framework of rule of law, *see* the Decision No. 70/18.4.2000 of the Constitutional Court of Romania, published in the Monitorul Oficial, Part I, No. 334/19.7.2000.
43. In reference to Art. 1, paras (4) and (5), *see* the following decisions of Constitutional Court: Decision No. 903/6.7.2010, published in the Monitorul Oficial, Part I, No. 584/17.8.2010; Decision No. 743/2.6.2011, published in the Monitorul Oficial, Part I, No. 579/16.8.2011; Decision No. 1/11.1.2012, published in the Monitorul Oficial, Part I, No. 53/23.1.2012; Decision No. 447/29.10.2013, published in the Monitorul Oficial, Part I, No. 674/1.11.2013; Decision No. 448/29.10.2013, published in the Monitorul Oficial, Part I, No. 5/7.1.2014; Decision No. 662/11.11.2014, published in the Monitorul Oficial, Part I, No. 47/20.1.2015; Decision No. 390/2.7.2014, published in the Monitorul Oficial, Part I, No. 532/17.7.2014; Decision No. 669/12.11.2014, published in the Monitorul Oficial, Part I, No. 59/23.1.2015; Decision No. 686/25.11.2014, published in the Monitorul Oficial, Part I, No. 68/27.1.2015; Decision No. 17/21.1.2015, published in the Monitorul Oficial, Part I, No. 79/10.1.2015 and so on.

§1. The Republican Aspect

21. In strictly formal terms, the republican ruling form was established after the abdication on 30 December 1947 of King Michael I and the instatement of the communist regime in Romania, when the first communist Constitution was adopted, on 13 April 1948, which abolished the monarchy and proclaimed the People's Republic of Romania. However, the totalitarian nature of the communist dictatorship altered the meaning of republican regime in its etymological sense of res publica, since the whole public, economic, cultural and social life of the country was reduced to the promotion of the interests of a ruling group. The establishment of a political oligarchy promoting an intransigent absolutism was in flagrant contradiction with the principles of republicanism. In other words, it was form without content, as there can be no substantial republican political regime without public freedoms and other inalienable human rights. The Communist Party became the sole party, present within every structure of the State, thus creating an authoritarian State, as well as a politically driven, centralized economy. For this reason, the republican ruling form, both in its strictly formal sense and in a substantial sense, was established only after the revolution of December 1989. In any case, it completely differs from what 'republic' used to mean during the communist regime. It is simply the difference between the false and the authentic. That is why when we speak of the Second Republic, we mean a republican regime totally different from the previous one and not an extension of it – unlike in France, for instance, where they speak of different republics in terms of the essence of the political regimes which consecrated them. All communist power structures (except for the army), namely the Presidency of the Republic, the Government, the State Council, the People's Councils, the Sole Party, and so on, were dissolved, thus allowing new, democratic structures to take over and make the changes required by a fast-changing world (and Europe).

§2. The National Aspect

22. A state bases its national character on its historical past, the cultural and spiritual community of the people and their common interests. In this respect, Article 4 provides that the State's foundation is the unity of the Romanian people and that Romania is the common and indivisible homeland of all its citizens, without any discrimination on account of race, nationality, ethnic origin, language, religion, sex, opinion, political adherence, property or social origin.[44] In this framework, according to Article 6 in the Constitution, the State recognizes and guarantees the right of persons belonging to national minorities to the preservation,

44. Provisions to be found in both the original text of 1991 and the revised text of 2003. We should mention the following related provisions: G.O. No. 137/2000, republished in the Monitorul Oficial, Part I, No. 166/7.3.2014; Law No. 202/2002, republished in the Monitorul Oficial, Part I, No. 326/ 5.6.2013.

development and expression of their ethnic, cultural, linguistic and religious identity.[45] That is why the national character of the State is in accordance with its democratic character.

§3. The Sovereign Aspect

23. Sovereignty as a concept includes both the principle of national sovereignty and that of popular sovereignty. In this respect, Article 2 of the Constitution provides that the national sovereignty resides with the Romanian people, who shall exercise it through their representative bodies and by referendum, and also that no group or person may exercise sovereignty in one's own name. Therefore, according to the Constitution, sovereignty is indivisible and inalienable, and its assignee is the people. The borders of the country are laid down by organic laws. The fundamental law enshrines the right to vote and its universal character, as well as some other democratic procedures – the constitutional referendum, the consultative referendum and the popular initiative.[46]

There are numerous consequences: precedence of Parliament within the framework of power separation, interdiction of the imperative mandate, immovability of elected persons, the republican form of governance, etc. It should be mentioned that the State's power may only be exercised within the constitutional limits on the functional competence of public authorities, as part of the principle of power separation within the State, and in observance of the international conventions to which Romania is a party and which, according to Article 11,[47] are part of the internal law and, according to Article 20, take precedence over the latter when human rights issues are at stake.[48]

45. *See also* the International Convention on the Elimination of all Forms of Discrimination, adopted by UN General Assembly by Resolution No. 2106 (XX), A/RES/20/2106, 21 Dec. 1965, which came into force on 4 Jan. 1969, to which Romania adhered by Decree No. 345/1970, published in the Monitorul Oficial, Part I, No. 92/28.7.1970; Framework Convention for the Protection of National Minorities adopted in Strasbourg, ratified by Romania by Law No. 33/1995, published in the Monitorul Oficial, Part I, No. 82/4.3.1995; the European Charter for Regional or Minority Languages adopted in Strasbourg on 5 Nov. 1992, ratified by Romania by Law No. 282/2007, published in the Monitorul Oficial, Part I, No. 752/6.11.2007.
46. The provisions of Art. 2 are in essence the same in the two texts, but in Art. 2 para. (1) states that the people's representative bodies 'result from free, periodical and fair elections, as well as by referendum' (*see* Irina Moroianu Zlătescu, *Constitutional Law: Romania – Text of the Constitution* (Wolters Kluwer, 2023), p. 17). *See also* the following laws: Law. No. 3/2000, published in the Monitorul Oficial, Part I, No. 84/24.2.2000; Law No. 370/2004, republished in the Monitorul Oficial, Part I, No. 650/12.9.2011; Law No. 35/2008, published in the Monitorul Oficial, Part I, No. 196/13.3.2008, *See also* Constitutional Court: Decision No. 682/27.6.2012, published in Monitorul Oficial Part I, No. 473/11.7.2012.
47. The revised text of 2003 includes an additional paragraph under Art. 11, para. 3, according to which 'If a treaty Romania is to become a party to comprises provisions contrary to the Constitution, its ratification shall only take place after the revision of the Constitution.' This paragraph was inspired by Romania's experience with the envisaged (at that time) adherence to the EU. The contradictions between the European legislation and certain provisions in the Constitution of 1991 were one of the reasons why the text of 1991 had to be revised.
48. *See* Irina Moroianu Zlătescu, *Codification in the Field of Human Rights*, in *Codification in International Perspective* (Springer International Publishing International Switzerland, 2014), p. 360.

§4. The Unitary Aspect

24. The unitary nature of the State results, mainly, from the fact that the country has a single legislative authority (Parliament), a single executive power, though with a twofold structure (the President of Romania and the Government), a single supreme judicial power (the High Court of Cassation and Justice), a single citizenship, and a single constitution. Territorial subdivisions have an exclusively administrative nature. At the external level, it is only the State that is a legal subject. It cannot be the object of a division. Not only is this structure the consequence of a historical evolution, but it also corresponds to the existence of a largely homogeneous population constituting a nation. For this reason, according to Article 152 in the revised text of 2003 paragraph 1 of the Constitution, (former Article 148 in the Constitution from 1991), the unitary and indivisible character of the State cannot be subject to a revision of the Constitution.[49]

§5. The Rule of Law

25. The rule of law principle is enshrined in Article 1 of the Constitution.[50] According to the Constitution, the rule of law principle means precedence of the law over the administration. No one – as Article 16 paragraph 2 of the Constitution[51] provides – can be above the law. In addition, this principle allowed the Constitution to further lay down the limits on the exercise of State power, the system and the essential aspects related to the status of public authorities through which this power is exercised, the sanctioning of the precedence of the Constitution – both through its rules of revision and, particularly, through the establishment of the control on the constitutionality of laws – and, especially, the preservation and safeguarding of the citizens' rights and fundamental freedoms, to mention only the main issues. The application of the rule of law principle is extremely vast. It is the basis of the constitutional status of political parties and trade unions, the national minorities' right to identity, the precedence of international guarantees regarding human rights, etc.

---

49. *See* the related regulations: Decision No. 799/17.6.2011 of the Constitutional Court of Romania, on Law Project regarding the revision of the Constitution, published in the Monitorul Oficial, Part I, No. 440/23.6.2011; Decision No. 80/16.2.2014, published in the Monitorul Oficial, Part I, No. 246/7.4.2014; Law No. 3/2000, published in the Monitorul Oficial, Part I, No. 84/24.2.2000.
50. In reference to this article, and also to the following articles, *see also* Cristian Ionescu, *Constituţia României. Legea de revizuire comentată şi adnotată cu dezbateri parlamentare* (Editura All Beck, Bucureşti 2003), pp. 14–20; Mihai Constantinescu et al., *Constituţia României revizuită: comentarii şi explicaţii* (Editura All Beck, Bucureşti, 2004), p. 8; Ioan Muraru and Elena Simina Tănăsescu, *Constituţia României. Comentariu pe articole* (Editura C.H. Beck, Bucureşti, 2008), pp. 10–12; Iancu, *Drept constituţional şi instituţii politice. Tratat., supra*, pp. 3 and the following; Cristian Ionescu, *Tratat de drept constituţional contemporan* (ed. 3, Editura C.H. Beck, Bucureşti), 2019; Ştefan Deaconu, *Drept constituţional* (Editura C.H. Beck, Bucureşti, 2022), pp. 3 and the following.
51. *See* G.O. No. 137/2000, republished in the Monitorul Oficial, Part I, No. 166/7.3.2014; Law No. 202/2002, republished din the Monitorul Oficial, Part I No. 326/5.6.2013, *see also* Art. 14 of the ECHR, as well as the Additional Protocol No. 12 of ECHR, Arts 20 and 21 of the CFREU. *See also* Irina Moroianu Zlătescu, *Şanse reale. Şanse egale* (*Equal Opportunities. Real Opportunities*) (Editura IRDO, Bucureşti, 1996), pp. 13–14.

§6. The Democratic and Social Aspect

26. According to the Constitution, the democratic and social character of the State implies the implementation of democratic principles for the governance of the country – the creation of representative authorities of the people only on the basis and under the control of elections, pluralism, the principle of majority, the protection of the opposition and of minorities in general, the guarantee for the citizens' rights and freedoms, the development of a semi-direct electoral machinery, etc. – as well as the State's social protection role for the most vulnerable segments of society. Intervention by the State at the economic level is not only required to guarantee social and economic rights but also the necessary consequence of its responsibility, as a result of its constitutional obligations, for effective policies of social security.

§7. Indivisibility

27. As comes out from Article 1, the political regime in Romania is a constitutional democracy. In this respect, paragraph 3 of Article 1 of the Constitution, while referring to such basic concepts as the rule of law and the democratic and social State, enshrines human dignity, the citizens' rights and freedoms, the free development of human personality, justice and political pluralism as supreme values that are constitutionally guaranteed. The principle of constitutional democracy implies the development of the democratic character of public life on the basis of and under the Constitution. Thus, democracy and the rule of law are synthesized in one and the same principle of constitutional democracy which, therefore, expresses and makes use of the exigencies of these two principles, their basic unity and their common purpose. That is why, as paragraph 1 of Article 8 of the Constitution provides, pluralism – political,[52] cultural, ethnic, linguistic, economic, etc. – represents a prerequisite for and a guarantee of constitutional democracy, since it allows the development of diversity and the assimilation of contradictions in the evolution of society. Therefore, constitutional democracy expresses unity in the diversity of the country's constitutional system.

Therefore, as Article 1 stipulates, Romania is a sovereign, independent, unitary and indivisible national State.

§8. Territorial Organization

28. Situated in the central and south-eastern part of Europe and covering an area of 237,500 sq. km, Romania has as its neighbours Ukraine in the north, the Republic of Moldavia and again Ukraine in the east, the Black Sea in the south-east, Bulgaria in the south, Serbia in the south-west, and Hungary in the west and north-west. Romania's present frontiers were established by the Peace Treaty concluded in Paris after World War II.

52. *See* the related provisions: Law No. 14/2003, republished in the Monitorul Oficial, Part I, No. 408/10.6.2015, Law No. 334/2006, republished in the Monitorul Oficial, Part I, No. 446/23.6.2015.

Romania's present configuration does not include a series of territories – Bessarabia in the East, Northern Bucovina, the county of Herţa – that were occupied in 1939 by the former Soviet Union following an ultimatum, after it had concluded the Molotov-Ribbentrop Pact with Germany. Part of these territories (Bessarabia) became the Republic of Moldavia, while the others were annexed to Ukraine. Also, the southern part of Dobrogea (the Quadrilateral) was ceded to Bulgaria as a result of the same Soviet-German treaty. Romania is made up of several historical provinces that have no administrative-territorial relevance: Muntenia (Walachia) and Oltenia in the south, Banat in the south-west, Crişana in the west, Maramureş in the north-west, Transylvania in the centre of the plateau bearing the same name (Southern) Bucovina in the north, Moldavia in the east, and Dobrogea in the south-east between the Danube and the Black Sea.

Communes, towns and counties are the units of the administrative-territorial organization. The Constitution stipulates that, as provided for by the law, some of the towns may be declared municipalities.

The county is the most important administrative-territorial unit. Romania's territory is organized into forty-one counties. The municipality of Bucharest, the State's capital with about 1,710,000 residents, within the greater metropolitan area of 2.31 million residents, one of the most populous cities by population within the limits of the EU, has the status of a county and is organized into six administrative sectors. Romania's other counties are the following: Alba, Arad, Argeş, Bacău, Bihor, Bistriţa-Năsăud, Botoşani, Braşov, Brăila, Buzău, Caraş-Severin, Călăraşi, Cluj, Constanţa, Covasna, Dâmboviţa, Dolj, Galaţi, Giurgiu, Gorj, Harghita, Hunedoara, Ialomiţa, Iaşi, Ilfov, Maramureş, Mehedinţi, Mureş, Neamţ, Olt, Prahova, Satu-Mare, Sălaj, Sibiu, Suceava, Teleorman, Timiş, Tulcea, Vaslui, Vâlcea, and Vrancea.

The main towns of the country, besides the capital, are: Arad, Braşov, Cluj-Napoca, Constanţa, Galaţi, Iaşi, Oradea, Ploieşti and Bacău, each having a population of about 300,000 inhabitants.

§9. Population

29. The latest census was scheduled to start in 2021, but due to the COVID-19 pandemic, it started on 1 February 2022. The last day of this process was 31 July 2022 and this was the first digitalized census (the thirteenth census in recorded history and the fourth after the 1989 Revolution). According to the National Institute for Statistics (INS), the official final and complete data became public by the end of 2023, showing that there are 19,053,815 resident individuals.[53]

53. (https://insse.ro/cms/ro/content/statistica-oficială-din-românia, accessed on 25 Oct. 2025) According to the latest finalized census, organized in 2022, Romania's population consisted of 19,053,815 individuals. This means that there was a certain decrease of the population owing to its low birth rate, the previous figures showing that there was a time when the population had exceeded 23,000,000 inhabitants. The great majority of the population is formed by the Romanians (14,801,442 inhabitants). The main minorities are the following: Hungarians (Szecklers included): 1,002,151 inhabitants; Gypsies: 569,477 inhabitants; Germans (Saxons and Swabians included): 22,907 inhabitants.

§10. Equality and Non-discrimination

30. Article 4 of the Constitution proclaims that Romania is the common and indivisible land of all its citizens, without any discrimination on account of race, nationality, ethnic origin, language, religion, sex, opinion, political adherence, property or social origin.[54]

In its Article 16, the Fundamental Act proclaims that citizens are equal before the law and public authorities, without any privilege or discrimination.

As a matter of fact, the prohibition of discrimination, which is a right asserted through negation – the right *not to be discriminated against*, is so important that it is reiterated three times after its first enshrinement under Article 4. Thus, it is mentioned for the second time under Article 6 (Right to identity), whose paragraph 2 provides that 'the protection measures taken by the Romanian State for the preservation, development and expression of identity of the persons belonging to national minorities shall conform to the principles of equality and non-discrimination in relation to the other Romanian citizens'. Then it is reiterated under Article 16, as was shown above, while Article 53, devoted to the restriction of certain rights or freedoms, provides in its second paragraph that 'such restriction shall only be ordered if necessary in a democratic society', while 'the measure shall be proportional to the situation having caused it, *applied without discrimination*, and without infringing on the existence of such right or freedom'.

54. *See* Irina Moroianu Zlătescu and Ioan Oancea, *Rights of the Persons Belonging to the National Minorities* (Regia Autonomă Monitorul Oficial, Bucureşti, 1993), p. 5; Irina Moroianu Zlătescu and Ioan Oancea, *The Legislative and Institutional Framework for the National Minorities of Romania* (Regia Autonomă Monitorul Oficial, Bucureşti, 1994), pp. 3 and the following; Irina Moroianu Zlătescu, *A Culture of Peace, Democracy and Tolerance in Romania* (National Commission of Romania for UNESCO, Editura IRDO, Regia Autonomă Monitorul Oficial, Bucureşti, 2002), pp. 149ff.; Irina Moroianu Zlătescu and Petru Emanuel Zlătescu, *Enforcement and Efectiveness and Antidiscrimination Law: Global Commonalities and Practices: Romania*, in *Comparative Perspective on the Enforcement and Efectiveness of Antidiscrimination Law* (Springer International Publishing, Switzerland, 2018), p. 415; Irina Moroianu Zlătescu, *Stadiul reglementării actuale pe plan internaţional a drepturilor persoanelor aparţinând minorităţilor naţionale*, în *Punctul critic* nr. 3 (25) (Editura Ideea Europeană, Bucureşti, 2018), pp. 159 and the following.

Chapter 2. Sources of Law

§1. Sources

31. After this brief presentation of a few facts related to Romania's history (mostly events that took place from the second half of the nineteenth century up to the present), its geographical position and the present-day structure of its population, a few considerations on the sources of the constitutional law could prove most useful to any analysis of a country's constitutional system.

In the formal meaning of the term, the sources of constitutional law are represented by the Constitution, international treaties and the law, as well as, in terms of these, by the jurisprudence of the Constitutional Court and other judicial bodies, by constitutional custom and parliamentary practice and by administrative acts of a normative character which are subordinated to the law. We shall deal with each of these sources, concluding with a brief examination of some particular aspects of the codification process and the interpretation and hierarchy related to the legal norms. This whole system of sources of the constitutional law results from the normative system established by the Constitution, or, in other words, from what has been defined by some authors as representing the normative constitutional law. The structure of the constitutional normative law results from the hierarchy of legal norms, which confer to the sources of law, generally, and to those of the constitutional law, particularly, a pyramidal structure with the Constitution at the top of the hierarchy, as a fundamental law. We are not going to deal with the features of the normative constitutional law, for they result from the very approach of its components. However, one aspect needs to be briefly presented first, as it is specific to the period of transition between the normative system of communist totalitarianism eliminated by the revolution of December 1989 and the new constitutional system established by the Constitution of 1991 and consolidated by its revised text of 2003.

32. A fundamental characteristic feature of any constitutional order is its uniqueness. This is the reason why any constitutional normative system should necessarily be unitary. The revolutionary overthrow of the previous communist system could not however be accompanied by the entire elimination of the laws instituted within this system. Undeniably, such a solution would have been clearly better, but it would have also been unrealistic, as it would have created a legislative vacuum certain to have negative effects upon the new constitutional order. Continuation of the national life required the avoidance of such a situation, so that the disruption represented by the establishment of the new constitutional order should not also result in a severe disruption of the national life. At the same time, however, survival, even partial, of the previous constitutional order and, therefore, of the normative system expressed by it is inconceivable. As already shown, the constitutional normative system cannot be but unitary, as the constitutional order expressing it is necessarily unique. For this reason, Article 154 paragraph 1 of the Constitution provides that the laws and all other normative acts shall remain in force in so far as they do not contradict the provisions of this Constitution.[55] This asserts both continuation of the national life as far as its juridical organization at the legislative level is concerned and the negative condition for accepting the previous, pre-constitutional law, that is, not to contradict the provisions of the Constitution; this latter condition also provides unity to the new constitutional normative system.

All the statements above are of special importance for the juridical system and, generally, the legislative system; they are of less importance, however, for the constitutional law as the latter results only from norms instituted after the revolution of December 1989 and, with some exceptions, based on the Constitution of 1991. By way of illustration, mention should be made in this respect of the norms regarding the establishment of political parties, the national anthem, and the standing orders of the Parliament's Chambers until revision, which were all pre-constitutional transitory regulations established after the revolution of December 1989.

33. It is generally agreed that the sources of the constitutional law are determined in terms of two cumulative criteria: *the organic criterion* of the authority passing it, which must be an authority of national representation, and *the material criterion* of the contents, according to which the norms of the constitutional law are related, in principle, to the fundamental rules regulating the process of establishing, maintaining and exercising power within the State. To be added to these are the subordinated or derived norms, such as those of jurisprudential, customary, administrative, etc., nature. This is so because, while detailing those belonging to the first category, they form together with them a unitary juridical structure or, in other words, a subsystem of the legislation and the normative system instituted by the Constitution.

34. As was said before, an important source of constitutional law is represented by treaties. Treaties – in a wider sense, international regulations – are sources of the constitutional law in terms of their contents, in so far as they refer to matters belonging to the area of the law. Two constitutional provisions are related to this particular aspect, namely, the provisions of Article 11,[56] according to which the treaties ratified by the Parliament are part of the national law, and the provisions of Article 20, according to which the constitutional provisions concerning the citizens' rights and liberties shall be interpreted and enforced in conformity with the Universal Declaration of Human Rights, with the covenants and other treaties Romania is a party to, and, where any inconsistencies exist between the covenants and treaties on fundamental human rights to which Romania is a party and internal laws, the international regulations shall take precedence, except for the cases when the Constitution or the national laws comprise more favourable provisions.

55. *See also* the Decision of the Constitutional Court of Romania, No. 38/7.7.1993, published in the Monitorul Oficial, Part I, No. 176/26.7.1993; the Decision of the Constitutional Court No. 545/5.7.2006, published in the Monitorul Oficial, Part I, No. 636/25.7.2006; the Decision of the Constitutional Court No. 498/10.5.2012, published in the Monitorul Oficial, Part I, No. 428/28.6.2012.
56. *See also* Moroianu Zlătescu, *Human Rights: A Dynamic and Evolving Process*, *supra*, 135.

Assimilating international law into domestic law, the text of Article 11 enshrines the principle of monism. By eliminating the dualism implied in the formerly existing shield of the law in the internal application of international regulations, the Constitution of 1991 enshrined the monistic principle of direct application of international regulations ratified by the Parliament as an internal law, thus providing unity of the Romanian public law from this point of view.

35. However, the provisions of Article 20 of the Constitution, as a source of the constitutional law, are more important, as they refer to the issue of the citizens' fundamental rights and freedoms. Since the constitutional status of the citizens, resulting mainly from their fundamental rights and freedoms, is one component of the constitutional law, the international regulations referring to these rights and freedoms implicitly define this status too. Thus, they express not only the national but also the international nature of the citizens' constitutional status regarding their fundamental rights and freedoms. The significance of Article 20 is triple. On the one hand, it lays down the obligation to interpret and apply fundamental rights and freedoms in accordance with the corresponding international regulations to which Romania is a party. Therefore, in this respect, Article 20 institutes a compulsory rule of interpretation. Taking into account the unity of the provisions referring to the fundamental rights and freedoms and the corresponding international provisions, Article 20 provides precedence in the interpretation of these rights and freedoms at the international level, the case law of the international courts of human rights included, in accordance with international practice and the practice of the bodies authorized to monitor and control the application of the respective regulations. Again, it is a monistic solution, seeking that one and the same right should not be differently interpreted at the national and the international levels, since its beneficiary, or, as the case may be, its holder, is one and the same person, namely, the citizen.

Another particularly important effect of the compulsory rule of interpretation laid down in Article 20 of the Constitution is the assimilation of the Universal Declaration of Human Rights as an internal norm. This Declaration is not a treaty or a convention, so its application at the national, internal level necessarily implies, as provided by Article 20, its constitutional interpretation as a directly applicable norm. The obligation to interpret the fundamental rights and freedoms in accordance with the corresponding international regulations is more than the rule enshrined by Article 11 of the Constitution, mentioned above, which refers to the direct assimilation of international law into internal law. This is so because a directly applicable international regulation, like a law, can derogate from earlier (international) regulations; whereas, when it comes to the issue of the fundamental rights and freedoms, the compulsory interpretation thereof in terms of the corresponding international regulation eliminates any possibility of deviation from the contents of these rights and freedoms, as defined at the international level. However, according to paragraph 3 added in 2003 to Article 11, in the case where a treaty Romania is to become a party to comprises provisions contrary to the Constitution, its ratification shall only take place after the revision of the Constitution.

36. On the other hand, a second meaning of Article 20 of the Constitution refers to the precedence of the international regulation in case it conflicts with an internal law. This precedence, like the previous compulsory rule of interpretation, refers exclusively to the fundamental rights and freedoms. Precedence of international regulations relating to human rights gives them an intermediate position, between the Constitution and the law. Since they are directly applicable, they oblige the judge or any other body that applies the law to eliminate a legal provision that contradicts the provisions of an international regulation on human rights in favour of the latter. Precedence of an international regulation in a conflict with the internal law implies an interpretative undertaking to determine the significance of this conflict; however, as a result of the constitutional precedence of the international regulation, the direct application of such a regulation is obligatory, together with the elimination of the conflicting internal law. The latter is eliminated not as contrary to the Constitution but as contrary to the international regulation. It is, therefore, a matter of applying the law in terms of the hierarchy of legal sources. It is a matter of legality, not constitutionality. Observation of the normative system established by the Constitution implies application of the specific sanction resulting from the hierarchy of this system, that is, the elimination of the law which is contrary to the higher rule.

The fact that international regulations on human rights have precedence over the internal regulations also provides dynamism to the internal development of these rights in terms of their evolution at the international level, of course, to the extent Romania becomes a party to these regulations. Taking into account the intermediate position of international regulations between the Constitution and the law, it appears that Romania's adherence to such regulations is conditioned by observance of constitutional provisions or, as the case may be, by prior revision thereof. Concluded on the basis of the Constitution, international treaties are a source of law of lower rank, so that they cannot contradict a constitutional provision.

37. Third, Article 20 of the Constitution states that the holders of rights and fundamental freedoms enjoy the benefit of not only the constitutional and legal safeguards of these rights and freedoms but also those established at the international level. However, the international safeguard is limited and conditioned by the international regulation that enshrines it.

This is the right place to reiterate that the text of Article 20 such as it was revised in 2003, introduced an amendment to the original version of 1991 to the effect that international regulations shall take precedence except for the cases when the Constitution or national laws comprise more favourable provisions.

To conclude, international regulations – treaties, conventions, protocols and other agreements to which Romania is party – are sources of constitutional law at the level of an enactment. They are directly applicable as internal law, with the exception of the international regulations on human rights which, having an intermediate position between the Constitution and the law, are a source of law superimposed upon internal law. This implies not only the compulsory interpretation of the rights and fundamental freedoms in accordance with their content but also the precedence of the international regulation conflicting with an internal law. Obviously, from this point of view, 'the law' has a large meaning; it refers not only to an act passed by the Parliament and promulgated by the President of Romania but also to any other subordinated act of a normative nature, such as Government decisions, ordinances, etc.

38. As was pointed out at the beginning of this monograph, Article 51 in the Constitution of 1991 was abrogated, while the principle contained in the respective text was worded identically under Article 1(5).

As laid down in this Article, the observance of the Constitution and of its supremacy is binding. Thus, observance of the Constitution and of its supremacy is instituted as a fundamental duty of the citizens, both as natural persons and in their capacity as members of social bodies, private or public.

Supremacy of the Constitution within the juridical system, understood as the sum total of legal norms – therefore as a normative system – as well as the sum total of the forms of expression of the legal norms – therefore as a legislative system, confers the Constitution a unique and central position. The unique position mainly results from the material meaning of the Constitution, according to which its object is to regulate the essential aspects of the exercise of the State's power, including towards the citizens. However, this position is also determined by the formal meaning, the organic criterion which appears from the procedural regulations for the adoption and modification of texts of a constitutional rank. From this point of view, the constitutional norms regulating the revision of the Constitution are of interest.

39. According to Article 150 in the Constitution of 2003, which fully reproduces the text of Article 146 in the Constitution of 1991, the initiative for the revision of the Constitution may be taken by the President of Romania at the proposal of the Government,[57] by a fourth of the total number of Deputies or Senators, or by the citizens, provided that 500,000 signatures have been obtained in favour of the revision, that these signatures come from at least half the number of the country's counties, and that at least 20,000 signatures have been obtained from each county. According to Article 151[58] in the Constitution of 2003 (former Article 147 in the Constitution of 1991), Constitutional laws are adopted by the Chamber of Deputies and by the Senate, by a majority of at least two-thirds of the members of each Chamber, and in the case of disagreement between the Chambers, by a three-quarters majority of the joint session of the two Chambers (such majority is a constitutional safeguard in favour of the Senate).

Following parliamentary adoption, the proposal is then submitted to the people for approval by means of a referendum (Article 153 in the Constitution of 2003, identical with Article 149 in the Constitution of 1991).

---

57. *See* the Decision of the Constitutional Court, No. 799/17.6.2011, published in the Monitorul Oficial, Part I, No. 440/23.6.2011.

58. In reference to this article, *see also* Law No. 3/2000 on the organization and conduct of the referendum, published in the Monitorul Oficial, Part I, No. 84/24.2.2000, most recently modified in 2023.

The above discussion about the material and the formal meaning of the Constitution concerns the uniqueness of its position within the juridical system. What follows concerns its central position within this system or, in other words, the supremacy of the Constitution within the normative system it has instituted.

40. Supremacy of the Constitution consists of the fact that all legal norms, consecrated by laws and normative acts subordinated to the law, should comply with the Constitution. From an institutional point of view, supremacy of the Constitution is mainly safeguarded by the duty of the Constitutional Court to eliminate from the legislation those normative acts which do not comply with it, as well as the role of the administrative courts to censor legality and, thereby, constitutionality of the public administration's acts. In this respect the law, both strictly (law in a formal sense, as an Act of Parliament promulgated by the President of Romania) and broadly (a general normative act, therefore also including regulations subordinated to the law) can only be instituted provided that it complies with the Constitution, both as far as procedures are concerned (such as competence rules) and substantially, that is, in terms of the contents of the regulation.

The direct application of the Constitution makes it the fundamental juridical act underlying the constitutional democracy, especially as it defines the fundamental elements of the citizens' status, as well as the fundamental public authorities, essential for the exercise of State power. Consequently, the Constitution ensures normatively and structurally the governance of the rule of law. In this respect, the constitutional safeguards for the exercise of the citizens' rights and freedoms, such as the plea of unconstitutionality, contentious matters falling within the competence of the administrative courts, the People's Advocate Institution, etc., are essential. All these aspects are merely mentioned here, but they will be dealt with in greater detail later on.

The Constitution cannot be modified except through a constitutional law adopted in observance of the constitutional provisions referring to this aspect. This provides high stability to the constitutional regime. Thus, supremacy of the Constitution is a normative constitutional safeguard of the citizens' rights and freedoms, all the more so as Article 152 paragraph 2 in the Constitution of 2003 (former Article 148 in the Constitution of 1991) provides that no revision shall be made if it results in the suppression of the citizens' fundamental rights and freedoms, or the safeguards thereof.[59]

41. The central position the Constitution holds within the juridical system has many consequences. They also include the hierarchy of the norms, which are subordinated to the Constitution: the law, regulations, etc. These aspects will be discussed later on, but, in principle, there is nothing peculiar about them as compared to the general hierarchy of the sources of law. However, supremacy of the Constitution has a different effect on the other branches of law, consisting of the constitutionalization of these branches of law. The essence of this process is that each

59. *See also* the Decision of the Constitutional Court, No. 799/17.6.2011, published in the Monitorul Oficial, Part I, No. 440/23.6.2011; the Decision of the Constitutional Court No. 80/16.2.2014, published in the Monitorul Oficial, Part I, No. 246/7.4.2014.

branch of law, be it the civil law or the administrative law, the commercial law or the tax law, the criminal law or the codes of procedures, etc., has a certain constitutional basis that more and more emanates from the interpretation of the constitutionality of its provisions. The constitutionalization process has two meanings:

1. The static meaning is that all legislation, irrespective of its level of organization, and all principles, institutions and provisions to be found in the texts of the laws, have to be founded on the provisions of the fundamental law. This implies development of an essential relationship between the Constitution and the provisions of the normative acts, none of the latter having any other justification except reference to the Constitution.
2. A second meaning, more dynamic, implies a deliberate 'constitutional purification' of the entire legislation and the elimination of all those provisions that are not rooted in the Constitution. It is, of course, the task of the Parliament and of other competent bodies to do such purification, but it is also the task of the constitutional, judicial and administrative institutions which, by doing a 'negative lawmaker's' work, eliminate provisions contradicting the Constitution.

42. Adoption of the Constitution of 2003 was a crucial moment and triggered a rapid process of penetration of the principles promoted by the Constitution both in the internal legislation and, more profoundly, in the practice of the judicial and administrative bodies, under the special circumstances of Romania's preparation for the Euro-Atlantic integration. This is obviously about integration of our country in the EU (as provided for under Article 148 in the Constitution of 2003), which took place on 1 January 2007, and its adherence to NATO (according to Article 149 in the Constitution of 2003), which took place on 29 March 2004, as was mentioned before.

The positive law, which comes second to the Constitution, is the most important source of constitutional law. While international regulations have an important but relatively reduced area of application, the positive law has a general voice. However, it is not only amplitude that determines the important position of positive law within the constitutional system but also, and particularly, the nature of certain categories of laws. According to Article 73 paragraph 1 of the Constitution of 2003 (Article 72 in the Constitution of 1991), laws are constitutional, organic, or ordinary. The first two categories have particular significance for constitutional law.

Laws are acts adopted in consonance by the two Chambers of the Parliament – the Chamber of Deputies and the Senate – according to the legislative procedure, and promulgated by the President of Romania. To this formal criterion, an implicit material criterion is to be added where constitutional laws are concerned: obviously, they must refer to revision of the Constitution. As regards organic laws, the material criterion is explicit and direct since they can only be adopted in those limited fields provided for such laws by the Constitution, as will be shown further.

§2. Constitutional Laws

43. It is the Parliament that adopts constitutional laws. These laws are, according to Article 73 in the Constitution of 2003, related to revision of the Constitution.

There are at least three reasons for the rigid nature characterizing the constitutional laws. First, the legislative initiative is limited, as already shown, to the President of Romania, on proposal by the Government, as far as the executive is concerned; to at least one-fourth of the total number of Deputies or Senators, as far as Parliament is concerned; as regards popular initiative, at least 500,000 citizens having the right to vote, coming from at least half the number of the country's counties, while each county, the municipality of Bucharest included, should have at least 20,000 signatures registered in support of the initiative (Article 150 in the revised Constitution of 2003, which reproduces the text of Article 146 in the Constitution of 1991).

A second reason is that revision should be adopted by at least two-thirds of each Chamber's members and, in case there is disagreement between the Chambers, by both Chambers in a joint session with a majority of at least three-quarters; once adopted, a revision is final only if approved by the voters through a referendum, organized within thirty days (Article 151 in the revised Constitution, which maintained the provision of Article 147 in the Constitution of 1991).

The third reason is that the provisions of the Constitution concerning the Republican system of government, territorial integrity, independence of the judiciary, political pluralism, official language, the citizens' fundamental rights and freedoms and the safeguards thereof shall not be subject to revision; at the same time, the Constitution shall not be revised during a state of siege or emergency, or during wartime (Article 152 in the Constitution of 2003, which reproduces the text of Article 148 in the Constitution of 1991).

As was pointed out by authors V.D. Zlătescu and M. Constantinescu in their comments on the Constitution of 1991,[60] rigidity of the Constitution represents the most important safeguard for the constitutional democracy, with regard to both the separation of and cooperation among powers within the State and the citizens' rights and fundamental freedoms.

§3. Organic Laws

44. Organic laws are characterized by three essential aspects: the restrictive nature of the circumstances under which an organic law can be adopted, the majority necessary for its adoption and the fact that the organic law implies a legislating area exclusively falling within the competence of the legislative branch, so that the fields it refers to cannot be the object of a legislative assignment granted by the Parliament. The first aspect is the result of the fact that the object of the organic law is

60. Mihai Constantinescu and Victor Dan Zlătescu, *Romania*, in *International Encyclopaedia of Laws* (gen. ed. Prof. Dr R. Blanpain, Kluwer Law International, 1996).

restrictively provided for by the Constitution. Article 73 paragraph 3 of the Constitution broadened the list of fields that shall be regulated by organic laws,[61] namely:

1. the electoral system; the organization and functioning of the Permanent Electoral Authority (the text referring to the organization and functioning of the Permanent Electoral Authority is a new text introduced by Article 73 in the revised Constitution of 2003);
2. the organization, functioning, and financing of political parties (the text of 1991 only mentioned the organization and functioning of political parties; the part referring to financing was introduced in 2003);
3. the statute of Deputies and Senators, the establishment of their emoluments and other rights (this is new text introduced in 2003; former paragraph (c) in the text of 1991 became paragraph (d) in the text of 2003, etc.);
4. the organization and holding of referendum;
5. the organization of the Government and of the Supreme Council of National Defence;
6. the state of partial or total mobilization of the armed forces and the state of war;
7. the state of siege and emergency;
8. criminal offences, penalties, and the execution thereof;
9. the granting of amnesty or collective pardon;
10. the statute of public servants;
11. the contentious business falling within the competence of administrative courts;
12. the organization and functioning of the Superior Council of Magistracy, the courts of law, the Public Ministry, and the Court of Audit;
13. the general legal status of property and inheritance;
14. the general organization of education;
15. the organization of local public administration, territory, as well as the general rules on local autonomy;
16. the general rules covering labour relations, trade unions, employers' associations, and social protection;
17. the status of national minorities in Romania;
18. the general statutory rules of religious cults; and
19. the other fields for which the Constitution stipulates the enactment of organic laws.

45. Various constitutional texts expressly provide that certain matters cannot be regulated but only by organic laws. There are some cases which we think are useful to enumerate:

1. consecration of the country's frontiers (Article 3, paragraph 2 – identical texts in the Constitution of 1991 and the revised Constitution of 2003);

61. *See also* the Decision of the Constitutional Court, No. 799/17.6.2011, published in the Monitorul Oficial, Part I, No. 440/23.6.2011; the Decision of the Constitutional Court No. 859/23.6.2011, published in the Monitorul Oficial, Part I, No. 639/7.9.2011.

2. acquiring, retaining and losing the Romanian citizenship (Article 5 paragraph 1 – identical texts in the Constitution of 1991 and the revised Constitution of 2003);
3. establishment of the country's coat-of-arms and seal (Article 12 paragraph 4 – identical texts in the Constitution of 1991 and the revised Constitution of 2003);[62]
4. organization of public radio and television services and the parliamentary control over their activity (Article 31 paragraph 5 – identical texts in the Constitution of 1991 and the revised Constitution of 2003);
5. establishment of some categories of public servants who may not join political parties (Article 37 paragraph 3 in the Constitution of 1991 and Article 40 paragraph 3 in the revised Constitution of 2003);
6. organization and functioning of the institution of People's Advocate Institution (Article 55 paragraph 1 in the Constitution of 1991 and Article 58 paragraph 3 in the revised Constitution of 2003);
7. establishment of other incompatibilities for Deputies and Senators other than those provided for by Article 68 of the Constitution (Article 68 paragraph 3 in the Constitution of 1991 and Article 71 paragraph 3 in the revised Constitution of 2003);
8. setting-up, organization and functioning of the Legislative Council (Article 79 paragraph 2 – identical texts in the Constitution of 1991 and the revised Constitution of 2003);
9. extension of the term of office of the President of Romania in the event of war or catastrophe (Article 83 paragraph 3 – identical texts in the Constitution of 1991 and the revised Constitution of 2003);
10. establishment of other Government members than the Prime Minister and the Ministers (Article 101 paragraph 3 in the Constitution of 1991 and Article 102 paragraph 3 in the revised Constitution of 2003);[63]
11. establishment of other incompatibilities of the office of member of the Government than those provided for by Article 104 paragraph 1 of the Constitution (Article 104 paragraph 2 in the Constitution of 1991 and Article 105 paragraphs 1 and 2 in the revised Constitution of 2003);[64]
12. establishment of autonomous administrative authorities (Article 116 paragraph 3 in the Constitution of 1991 and Article 117 paragraph 3 in the revised Constitution of 2003);[65]
13. establishment of the structure of the national defence system, the organization of the Army, the preparation of the population, economy and territory for defence purposes, as well as the status of the military (Article 117 paragraph 2 in the Constitution of 1991 and Article 118 paragraph 2 in the revised Constitution of 2003);

62. It is worth mentioning that, in this respect, Law No. 146/2016 amending Law No. 102/1992 on Romania's coat-of-arms and seal was promulgated on 12 Jul. 2016, published in the Monitorul Oficial, Part I, No. 542/19.7.2016.
63. *See* the Administrative Code, adopted by GEO No. 57/2019, published in the Monitorul Oficial, Part I, No. 555/5.7.2019, amended and supplemented.
64. *Ibid.*
65. *Ibid.*

14. organization of the police and the security services of the State, as well as the other components of the Armed Forces, and the status of military personnel (Article 117 paragraph 3 in the Constitution of 1991 and Article 118 paragraph 3 in the revised Constitution of 2003);[66] and
15. organization and functioning of the Constitutional Court (Article 140 paragraph 4 in the Constitution of 1991 and Article 142 paragraph 5 in the revised Constitution of 2003).

While according to the Constitution of 1991, extension of the mandate of the Chamber of Deputies and the Senate in case of war or catastrophe was to be regulated by an organic law (Article 60 paragraph 1), according to the revised Constitution of 2003, the term of office of four years may be extended de jure in the event of a mobilization, war, siege, or emergency, until such event has ceased to exist (Article 63, paragraph 1).

46. Other modifications and/or new provisions introduced in the text of the revised Constitution of 2003 in relation to the organization and the administration of justice, which shall be regulated by organic laws, include:

1. the role of a court of law performed by the Superior Council of Magistracy by means of its sections, as regards the disciplinary liability of judges and public prosecutors, based on the procedures set up by its organic law – cases when the Minister of Justice, the president of the High Court of Cassation and Justice, and the general Public Prosecutor of the Public Prosecutor's Office attached to the High Court of Cassation and Justice shall not be entitled to vote (Article 134 paragraph 2);
2. the text of paragraph 4 under Article 134, according to which the Superior Council of Magistracy shall also perform other duties stipulated by its organic law, in order to accomplish its role of guarantor for the independence of justice, is also new as compared to the text of 1991;
3. the composition of the High Court of Cassation and Justice, and the regulation for its functioning shall be set up in an organic law (Article 126 paragraph 4);
4. the provisions of paragraph 5 under Article 126, according to which it is prohibited to establish extraordinary courts of law, while courts of law specialized in certain matters may be set up by means of an organic law, allowing the participation, as the case may be, of persons outside the magistracy;
5. the right of the Romanian citizens belonging to national minorities to express themselves in their mother tongue before the courts of law, under the terms of the organic law (Article 128 paragraph 2);
6. the conditions under which public property may be administered, granted, or leased (Article 136 paragraph 2);

---

66. *See* Law No. 45/1.7.1994 on national defense, published in the Monitorul Oficial, Part I, No. 172/7.7.1994, modified by Law No. 58/29.4.2011, published in the Monitorul Oficial, Part I, No. 303/3.5.2011. *See also* Law No. 291/2007, on the status of foreign armed forces on the Romanian territory, republished in the Monitorul Oficial, Part I, No. 321/5.5.2014, updated in 2023.

7. acknowledgement and replacement of the national currency by that of the EU (Article 137 paragraph 2);
8. the provisions referring to the Court of Audit, the appointment and the revocation of the audit advisers (Article 140 paragraphs 1, 5 and 6);[67]
9. the establishment by the revising Law No. 429/2003 of the Economic and Social Council, by Article 141, which 'shall be an advisory body of the Parliament and the Government, in the specialized fields stated by the organic law for its establishment, organization and functioning';[68]
10. the conditions for the periodic and partial renewal of the Constitutional Court (Article 142 paragraph 5); and
11. fulfilment of other powers by the Constitutional Court in case of new situations, correlating the dynamism of the law to that of social life, without violating the Constitution (Article 146 paragraph e).[69]

This enumeration reflects that the main criterion to define organic laws is the material one. Importance of the regulation, not only for the organization and exercise of power within the State but also for issuing laws related to other fields of activity, was the essential criterion by which the Constitution assigned fields to be regulated by organic laws. In terms of constitutional law, the material criterion is of a special nature because, within this branch of law, the organic law represents an extension and detail rendering of the Constitution. Not all the fields dealt with by organic laws are of interest to constitutional law. However, organic laws which provide more details concerning some constitutional provisions are an extension thereof in this respect. By way of illustration, we mention here the electoral system, the organization and functioning of the Permanent Electoral Authority, the organization, functioning and financing of political parties, the organization and holding of a referendum, the statute of Deputies and Senators and the establishment of their emoluments and other rights (former Article 72, now Article 73 paragraph 3 items a–d of the Constitution), mandate extension for the President of Romania (Article 83 paragraph 3 of the Constitution), establishment of other incompatibilities for Parliament members or Government members than those provided for by the Constitution (Article 68 paragraph 3 and Article 102 paragraph 3 of the Constitution), organization and functioning of the Constitutional Court (Article 142 paragraph 5 of the Constitution), etc.

47. As far as the legislative procedure is concerned, according to Article 76 paragraph 1, organic laws shall be passed by a majority vote of the members of each of the two Chambers in a joint session.

Article 75 in the Constitution is based on a new concept. It maintains equality of the two Chambers, but they are differentiated into a decisional Chamber and a

---

67. Functioning according to Law No. 94/1992, republished in the Monitorul Oficial, Part I, No. 238/ 3.4.2014.
68. Functioning according to Law No. 109/2.7.1997, published in the Monitorul Oficial, Part I, No. 141/ 7.7.1997, updated and supplemented.
69. Functioning according to Law No. 47/18.5.1992, republished in the Monitorul Oficial, Part I, No. 807/3.12.2018, amended by Law No. 168/2018.

reflective Chamber. The Chamber of Deputies has the role of a decisional Chamber of common law when the decisional competence lies with the Senate. The latter has the competence of decisional Chamber for the ratification of treaties and other agreements, as well as legislative measures resulting from their application; also, in the field of organic laws that exclusively deal with the organization and functioning of the State.

As already shown, the organic law implies a legislating area exclusively falling within the competence of the legislature. This feature appears from the provisions of Article 115 paragraph 1 of the Constitution, according to which legislative delegation is allowed only in fields outside the scope of organic laws.

§4. Ordinary Laws

48. As a source of constitutional law, ordinary laws are less important than the organic laws. The only constitutional provision that refers to such a law and is of interest as far as constitutional law is concerned is Article 73 of the Constitution regarding the emoluments and other rights to which the members of the Parliament are entitled. Of course, this does not mean that an ordinary law could not also regulate other aspects belonging to the field of constitutional law; nevertheless, as has been shown, the main source of law, apart from the Constitution, is organic laws. One exception, however, to be pointed out, given the role played by the Parliament's Standing Orders in the field of parliamentary law, is a component of constitutional law. An expression of the autonomy of the Chambers which, according to Article 64 paragraph 1 of the Constitution, is a constitutional principle, the Standing Orders regulate the establishment, organization and functioning of the working bodies of the Chambers – the President, the Parliament's Commissions (standing, special, investigating, mediation, etc., committees), the political structure of the Chambers – the parliamentary groups, the conducting and development of the sessions as well as other aspects of the parliamentary procedure. The latter includes participation of the members of Parliament in the sessions, particularly those related to the expression of opinions, the right to bring and the procedure for amendments (the right to propose amendments is provided not by the Constitution but by the Standing Orders), the voting procedure, the departments of the Chambers, etc. The special importance of the Parliament's Standing Orders – for the Chamber of Deputies, the Senate, and the joint session – is given by the fact that, since they represent Parliament's internal law within the constitutional limits of parliamentary autonomy, they are subordinated directly to the Constitution and are, just like organic laws, an extension and expansion thereof. For this reason, according to Article 76 of the Constitution, they are adopted by an absolute majority vote of the members of each Chamber, and in case of Standing Orders of joint sessions, also by the vote of the two Chambers gathered in joint session. It is for this reason that the Parliament's Standing Orders represent an essential normative act characteristic of parliamentary democracy.

Therefore, the law as a source of constitutional law is of major importance, particularly as far as constitutional laws and organic laws are concerned: the former because its effect is the revision of the constitutional regime; the latter because it is an extension, a practical application, and an expansion of this regime. Similar to organic laws are the Parliament's Standing Orders that, within the limits of the constitutional principle of Parliament's ruling autonomy, provide, as far as its organization and functioning are concerned, the expansion and practical application of the constitutional provisions, representing the internal law for the sessions of Parliament.

49. As was pointed out at the beginning of the discussion on the sources of constitutional law, another important source is the jurisprudence and it is the jurisprudence of the Constitutional Court that is of particular interest to constitutional law. All of the Constitutional Court's powers give it competence. These powers include: the preventive, prior to promulgation, control of a law passed by Parliament; the preventive control of the treaties or other international agreements, also prior to their promulgation; the *a posteriori*, after promulgation control of Parliament's Standing Orders; the *a posteriori* control, after promulgation and publication in the Monitorul Oficial of Romania of an organic or an ordinary law, as well as Government's ordinances, by means of a plea of unconstitutionality; the resolution of legal conflicts, of constitutional nature, between authorities. The above-mentioned powers are exercised on intimation by the subjects stipulated under paragraphs (a)–(e) of Article 146, where the text of 2003 added the People's Advocate Institution in paragraph (a) and the People's Advocate (d), the President of Romania, one the presidents of the two Parliamentary Chambers, the Prime Minister and the president of the Superior Council of Magistracy in paragraph (e).[70] The Constitutional Court also exercises other powers including: controls ex officio the initiatives for the revision of the Constitution; the control on the observance of the procedure for the election of the President of Romania and confirmation of the suffrage results; acknowledges the interim of the President of Romania office and communicates it to Parliament and the Government; issues an advisory opinion on the proposal for the President of Romania's suspension from office; monitors the observance of the referendum procedure and the confirmation of the result; monitors the legality and constitutionality of the citizens' legislative initiatives; solves the challenge against the constitutionality of a political party.

There are two main aspects characterizing the Court's jurisprudence as a source of law. The first one refers to the Court's capacity of 'negative legislator' since, when found unconstitutional, a text becomes inapplicable as a result of the general binding nature of the Court's decisions under Article 147 of the Constitution. Consequently, as a result of the *a priori* control, the law shall be forwarded for promulgation without the text that was declared unconstitutional or shall not be forwarded at all if it was declared unconstitutional as a whole, with the only reserve that the

70. Article 146: 'The Constitutional Court shall have the following powers: a) to adjudicate on the constitutionality of laws, before the promulgation thereof upon notification by the President of Romania, one of the presidents of the two Chambers, the Government, the High Court of Cassation and Justice, the People' Advocate Institution, a number of at least fifty deputies or at least twenty-five senators, as well as ex officio, on initiatives to revise the Constitution; … (e) to solve legal disputes of a constitutional nature between public authorities, at the request of the President of Romania, one of the presidents of the two Chambers, the Prime Minister, or of the president of the Superior Council of Magistracy.

two Chambers of Parliament may, according to the re-examination procedure, adopt the law in its initial form, by a majority of two-thirds. With the *a posteriori* control of the law or of the Parliament's Standing Orders, such an exception is not provided for, and so the decision by the Court is unconditionally applicable. The second aspect refers to interpretative decisions which eliminate the possibility of giving the text of a law an interpretation contrary to the Constitution and provide an interpretation that becomes compulsory, since the constitutionality of the law depends on it.

Either way, the Court's decisions are a source of law as they result either in the failure to apply a law or a provision of a law, or in the application thereof in the interpretation given by the Court. Since every decision by the Court is based on the interpretation of a constitutional norm, it is implicitly a source of law not only for the law branches to which the respective law refers, with a constitutionalization effect on those branches, but also for the constitutional law itself, as it is a matter of understanding and applying the Constitution.

50. The jurisprudence of courts other than the Constitutional Court is also of interest to constitutional law. This concerns not only the jurisprudence of the High Court of Cassation and Justice and, particularly, the law on appeal, which, by providing a uniform interpretation, is a jurisprudential source of law but also the constants of judicial practice, particularly those disputed matters falling within the competence of the administrative courts which provide judicial control of administrative acts, those of a normative nature included. The Constitution being directly applicable, the court is bound to give such an interpretation to the texts applicable for the resolution of the litigation that is compliant with the provisions of the Constitution. That is why, when checking an administrative act for legality, it also considers whether it was not issued using 'excess of power', that is, by violating the normative system established by the Constitution. However, in case the problem of constitutionality of the law arises, the court is bound to intimate the Constitutional Court by the plea of unconstitutionality, no matter whether it was raised by the parties or ex officio by the judges.

Given that the constitutionality of laws falls within the competence of the Constitutional Court, and administrative acts subject to judicial control in general are not related to this branch of law, judicial practice has no particular importance for constitutional law. There are, however, some exceptions, such as those related to electoral disputes in general and local elections where the courts have an essential role, or those related to the control of the legality of an ordinance, of course, in so far as it refers to a constitutional matter. Ordinances are subject to the jurisdiction of the Constitutional Court, but they can also be attacked before the administrative court since, being issued by the Government, they are an administrative act of a normative nature. Of course, if they were approved by Parliament, ordinances are merely a legislative act and, like any law, can only be attacked before the Constitutional Court.

What has been said above in relation to jurisprudence leads to the conclusion that it is undoubtedly a secondary source of law whose importance mostly lies in the fact that it provides the interpretation of the Constitution for the resolution of the litigations brought before the courts. In this respect, an important role is played by the jurisprudence of the Constitutional Court within the framework of the control on the constitutionality of laws, Parliament's Standing Orders, and ordinances issued on the basis of an authorizing law.

§5. Customary Law

51. The judicial doctrine on constitutional law in Romania has generally recognized that custom has a role as a source of law, especially by generalization of some constitutional practices compliant with the provisions of the fundamental law or which compensate for certain gaps or inaccuracies. However, a custom abrogating or opposed to the provisions of the Constitution is questionable. Theoretically, it is not accepted by the doctrine.

As a matter of fact, there are certain practices which, by repetition, could acquire the value of a custom. Thus, by way of illustration, we mention the message presented by the President of Romania before the Chambers gathered in joint session after the oath-taking, and the practice of consultation of the President of Romania with the parties represented in the Parliament in order to establish a political dialogue in case of a locked vote or rejection of a law as a result of the re-examination procedure based on a decision by the Constitutional Court which goes beyond the effects of this decision. The practice of having representatives of the trade unions participate in the debates within the parliamentary Commission on drafts of law concerning their activity has the same significance. Nevertheless, even with such aspects, it is only after a longer period of time that one will be able to see whether they have the value of a customary norm or whether they are mere circumstantial solutions, related to the personal style of certain political actors.

52. The Constitution recognizes custom under Article 44 paragraph 7 in relation to the duties of property: The right of property compels the observance of duties relating to environmental protection and ensures neighbourliness, as well as other duties incumbent upon the owner, in accordance with the law or custom. For this reason, in principle, it is part of the constitutional normative system, so that there is no reason why it should not be accepted in the field of constitutional law, where the specific Romanian constitutionalism has always recognized its creative effect. It asserted itself not only within the framework of the relationship between public authorities but particularly in parliamentary practice through the non-application or application of the Standing Orders.

To exemplify, it is worth mentioning here that the final vote regarding a law had originally been a parliamentarian custom before it was legislated under the Standing Orders, while the present practice of adopting organic laws by a simple majority with an article-by-article ballot, and by absolute majority, as required by the Constitution, with the final ballot is also a parliamentarian custom.

§6. Normative Acts Subordinated to the Law

53. Ordinances, resolutions, decisions, directions, methodological norms, etc., are all normative acts subordinated to the law. Generally, their importance as a source of constitutional law is small, and part of the doctrine, while bearing in mind the object of constitutional law – fundamental social relations in the establishing, maintaining and exercising of power within the State – even considers that such acts could not be sources of constitutional law since they are not passed by a representative body of the people. Even if the objection was raised that the President of Romania is such a body, the argument is not acceptable since the President may not pass normative acts: the promulgation of laws and the signing of treaties in the name of Romania are not considered to be such acts. The Government has an indirect popular legitimacy, since it has parliamentarian roots. For this reason, we consider that its acts – ordinances and Government decisions – could be a derived source of constitutional law, provided they are issued for the execution of a normative act such as a law or the Constitution. Obviously, it depends on the issue to be regulated, on its importance for the constitutional regime, and on its influence in the exercise of power. While adopting a reserved attitude as to whether they are a source of constitutional law or not, we are going to briefly deal with the two main categories of acts subordinated to the law: ordinances and Government decisions.

54. The Constitution provides that Parliament can adopt a special law enabling the Government to issue ordinances in fields outside the scope of organic laws. Legislative delegation is one kind of cooperation between Parliament and the Government, on the basis of the principle of separation and collaboration among powers within the State. Through delegation, the Government is vested with the power to exercise, under certain circumstances, a legislative function. Such delegation of power can be granted only by law because it goes beyond the Government's primary competence, which is limited to the execution of laws. It should be pointed out from the very beginning that such a measure may only be taken in relation to matters that can be regulated by ordinary laws.

There are certain requirements that delegation should meet. Thus, it shall be accurately determined in terms of its object, and it shall be limited in time as well. Article 115 paragraph 2 of the Constitution provides that the enabling law shall compulsorily establish the field and the date up to which ordinances can be issued. Delegation is an exceptional measure and it is for this reason that it cannot be granted unconditionally. Usually, ordinances issued on the basis of delegation are not bound to be later subject to Parliament's approval. It is only when the enabling law expressly requires such approval that it becomes necessary. The ordinance shall in that case be submitted to Parliament for approval by the end of the enabling term; non-compliance with the term entailing, according to Article 115 paragraph 3 of the Constitution, discontinuation of effectiveness of the ordinance.

Paragraphs 4 and 5 of Article 115 provide that in exceptional cases the Government may adopt emergency ordinances, an institution of legislative delegation, even without previous enabling by the legislature. The explanation is that, in exceptional circumstances, Parliament may not be in a position to convene, not even for adopting an enabling law nor for making use of the rapid procedure. It has been claimed in the literature that, in such cases, restriction of the right to issue ordinances in the field of ordinary laws would be inoperative and, therefore, such speedy ordinances can also be issued in the field of organic laws. Such a thesis can find support in the wording of paragraph 1 of Article 115, which provides that the enabling law can only be adopted by Parliament in fields outside the scope of organic laws. As paragraph 5 under Article 115 provides, *an emergency ordinance containing norms of the same kind as the organic law must be approved by a majority stipulated under Article 76 (1)*, that is, 'the majority vote of the members of each Chamber', not the majority vote of the members *present* in each Chamber. On the contrary, when ordinances are not issued on the basis of an enabling law, the field is not restricted at all.

It has to be pointed out that, if not issued on the basis of an enabling law, emergency ordinances become effective only after submission for parliamentary approval. If Parliament is not in session, it shall be compulsorily convened within five days after submittal or, as the case may be, after forwarding. If, within thirty days at the latest of the submitting date, the notified Chamber does not pronounce on the ordinance, the latter shall be deemed adopted and shall be sent to the other Chamber, which shall also make a decision in an emergency procedure.

Apparently, paragraph 5 under Article 115 includes two time limits. The first one refers to the submittal of the ordinance to the competent Chamber for debate in an emergency procedure, while the second one refers to publication in the Monitorul Oficial of Romania. This is in fact just an appearance because the logical interpretation of the text, corroborated with a systematic interpretation of the Constitution, leads to a conclusion according to which it is inconceivable that an emergency ordinance be published in the Monitorul Oficial of Romania before having been submitted to the competent Chamber for debate.

In case Parliament rejects an ordinance issued on the basis of an enabling law, its effects shall cease starting with the date when the rejection law is published. Similarly, if it is modified during the approval procedure, it shall be applied in its modified form starting with the same date. If it is passed, the ordinance is given the status of a law.

55. According to the Constitution, the Government also has a normative competence of its own, which is not just the result of a legislative delegation and which has a constitutional basis. This competence is exercised through the decision which, according to Article 108 of the Constitution, shall be issued to organize the execution of laws. A decision is, by excellence, an act by means of which the Government exercises its constitutional role regarding the general management of public administration. Having a general material competence, it can issue decisions in any field, branch or sector of activity.

It is extremely important to point out that the Government's decisions can only be *secundum legem* and *praeter legem.* The need for a decision and its legitimacy can only be estimated to the extent that the execution of certain provisions of the law demands subsequent measures or rules. The issuing of a decision may be provided for by the law; however, nothing prevents the Government from adopting decisions, even though they are not provided for by the law, in case execution of the latter requires it.

In its capacity as an administrative act, a Government's decision, just like an ordinance, can be attacked before the administrative court prior to coming into effect.

The analysis of the constitutional law sources should be followed by a discussion about the codification, the interpretation and the hierarchy of legal norms, which are three important aspects for the characterization of the evolution of these sources.

It is most important to streamline and systematize the sources of law within a unitary regulation that avoids overlaps and possible contradictions owed to the time sequence of laws, as well as legislative gaps or other uncertainties that could have a negative impact on the process of ruling social relations. This is what codification does.

56. As far as Romania is concerned, codification is particularly characteristic of the private law and especially of criminal law, though, even in this field, the streamlining process has been negatively influenced by excessive legislative development. There are some proposals for codification – a code of minor offences, an administrative code – which, however, have not so far been adopted by the public authorities, either the Government or Parliament. For this reason, codification is not characteristic of the development of the sources of law. At the same time, the Romanian legislative practice has known no procedure of codification consisting of an official compilation of texts originating in different sources, in order to ensure their unitary application. The only codification made use of was inclusion of the regulations regarding a certain field into a new, systematized, regulation.

As was pointed out before, interpretation of the Constitution by the Constitutional Court in the process of the control of the constitutionality of laws, the Parliament's Standing Orders and the Government's ordinances is of the utmost importance. These aspects have already been mentioned in the discussion on jurisprudence as a source of constitutional law. For this reason, we shall confine ourselves to merely pointing out that the importance of such interpretation lies not only in that it is given by a unique authority of constitutional jurisdiction and that it regards the Constitution itself and the constitutional legitimacy of the law but also that, according to Article 147 paragraph 4 of the Constitution, the Constitutional Court's decisions are binding once published in the *Monitorul Oficial of Romania* and shall have effect only for the future.

57. When speaking about the hierarchy of the sources of law, one has to bear in mind that the normative system instituted by the Constitution has a pyramidal structure, with the Constitution at the top. Normative acts stand below the Constitution and are hierarchically structured as follows: (a) normative acts directly subordinated to the Constitution, constitutional law, organic or ordinary laws (this framework also includes international conventions, since they are approved by law); (b) ordinances, within the limits of legislative delegation; (c) normative acts issued for the application of the law, Government decisions, decrees, orders, directions, methodological norms and other acts issued by the various authorities of the central or local public administration; their hierarchy shall be established in terms of the authority of the issuing body.

The relationship between the Constitution and the acts directly subordinated to it is of particular interest for constitutional law because the acts for the application of the law are characteristic of the field of administrative law. Supremacy of the Constitution over the normative acts directly subordinated to it is provided by the control of constitutionality of laws, Parliament's Standing Orders and Government ordinances. As a result of the provisions of Article 1 paragraph 5 in the Constitution of 2003 (former Article 51 in the text of 1991) regarding the obligation to observe the supremacy of the Constitution, and Article 14 of the Constitution regarding the binding nature of the Constitutional Court's decisions, a legal provision declared unconstitutional is inapplicable. As regards the institutional aspects of the control of constitutionality, they will be analysed below. We shall here confine ourselves to pointing out that such control provides observance of the hierarchy of the normative acts instituted by the Constitution within the framework of the judicial system.

The hierarchy of normative acts in the relationship between the law and the acts subordinated to it, as well as among the latter, falls within the competence of courts, particularly the administrative courts. It is a consequence of the normative system instituted by the Constitution, not as a source of law of jurisprudential nature as, from this point of view, it belongs to the field of administrative law. The hierarchy of the legal norms reflects the hierarchy of the authorities that have adopted them. Thus, the constitutional law is the act of the derived constituent power, being adopted by the Parliament and approved by the people by means of a referendum. The organic or ordinary law is the act of the Parliament, as the unique law-making body in the country. This is why it is passed, in this form, by the two Chambers of Parliament, on mutual agreement, and is promulgated by the President of Romania. The difference between these two categories of laws mainly consists in the majority needed for the law to be passed – absolute for the organic law and relative for the ordinary law – as well as in that the organic law is determined not only in terms of a formal criterion, applicable to any category of laws but also in terms of a material criterion, which contours a limited area that exclusively belongs to the legislator. The ordinance is a governmental act, the expression of the legislative delegation conferred by law, exclusively limited to what can constitute the field of an ordinary law or, in the case of emergency ordinances, directly by the Constitution. Once passed by the Parliament, an ordinance becomes a law. The Government decision represents an act for the application of a law as an expression of an authority with general competence, both materially and territorially. The other normative acts subordinated to the law have the juridical power conferred by the specific authority of the issuing body, that is, restricted to its functional field or area. At the local level, this will be the authority of the bodies of the local public administration, the Mayor and the Local Council, within the administrative-territorial unit where it operates: commune, town, municipality or county.

Part II. System of Government

Chapter 1. Generalities

58. The Constitution of 1991 instituted the political regime of a parliamentary republic of a dualistic type since there are two main power pillars within the State: the Parliament and the President of Romania. It is, however, a political regime different from the dualism of the classical parliamentary regimes, since the executive is not monistic but bicephalous, the President of Romania having his own representativeness that results from his election by the people, while the Government has an indirect one, as a result of its parliamentary origin. These features originate from the following principles.

Both the Parliament and the President of Romania, who is the Head of State, are public authorities elected by universal suffrage. For this reason, their legitimacy comes directly from the popular suffrage while they are representative bodies of the nation through whom, as provided by Article 2 of the Constitution, the nation exercises its sovereignty, internally and externally. These provisions in the Constitution of 1991 are also to be found in the text of the Constitution of 2003 (Article 2).

According to Article 61 paragraph 1 of the Constitution, Parliament is the supreme representative body of the people. In this respect, it is the only legislative authority of the country; it validates the Government by passing its vote of confidence or invalidates it by withdrawing its confidence, it exercises the parliamentary control of the executive, as well as in any social field, etc. Accordingly, the Government has a parliamentary origin and is politically responsible for its entire activity only before the Parliament.

59. As Article 80 in the Constitution stipulates, the President of Romania 'shall represent the Romanian State and is the safeguard of the national independence, unity and territorial integrity of the country'. Also, he 'shall guard the observance of the Constitution and the proper functioning of the public authorities. To this effect, he shall act as a mediator between the Powers in the State, as well as between the State and society'. As part of the executive, it exercises the powers provided for by the Constitution. These powers give him a competence shared either with the Government which, in certain cases, is entitled to initiate certain acts or, for the acts countersigned by the Prime Minister, assumes political responsibility, or with the Parliament regarding the powers that he may exercise only on the prior or later approval by the Parliament. At the same time, the President of Romania also exercises an exclusive competence, often of a prevailing political character: mediation between the powers within the State and between the State and society, designation of the candidate for the office of Prime Minister, promulgation of laws and request for re-examination of a law prior to promulgation, intimation of the Constitutional Court by an objection of unconstitutionality prior to the promulgation of a law, consultation of the people by means of a referendum, consultation of Government members and participation, in particular cases, in the meetings of the Government, dissolution of Parliament under the conditions provided for by the Constitution, etc. The President also has some conditioned competencies, such as appointment of Government members on the basis of a confidence vote passed by the Parliament and the compulsory promulgation of a law whose constitutionality has been established by the Chambers of Parliament.

Nevertheless, the shared and exclusive competencies are determinative for the presidential office. Through them, the President has an active role and not a merely symbolic one. In accordance with the legitimacy he enjoys as a result of his election by popular suffrage, the President of Romania is, as part of the executive, an active and important political actor, particularly during periods of crisis and for the resolution of conflicts – although this is also true under normal circumstances as a result of his collaboration with the Government and his cooperation with the Parliament, mainly by means of presidential messages and the requests for re-examination of laws prior to promulgation.

As the President appoints the judges and the prosecutors on proposal by the Superior Council of Magistracy, it comes out that one of the presidential competences is related to the judiciary. Since he is elected directly by the people, the President is not politically responsible to the Parliament; the latter, however, may suspend him from office in case of grave acts infringing upon constitutional provisions, or may pass a resolution for his impeachment for high treason. These two cases have an exceptional character and represent judicial, not political, responsibility. The presidential office is based on its legitimacy resulting from the direct election of the President by the people, and it is only the latter which, after his suspension from office, may dismiss him.

60. While the classical parliamentary dualism is characterized by the fact that the Government is responsible to the Head of State who appointed it, the dualism of the parliamentary regime in Romania is characterized by the existence of two public authorities elected directly by the people – the Parliament and the President of Romania – which exercise the national sovereignty in their capacity as representative bodies of the people, each having its own constitutional position and distinct competence. Although the Parliament has a supreme position, being the supreme representative body of the people and the unique legislative authority of the country, the President of Romania is an active political actor, not a mere symbol, with a more formal function. As a result of his election and ensuing legitimacy, the position and the role of the President of Romania, by contrast with those of the Head of State in a parliamentary republic, theoretically justify, not only judicially but also politically, the definition of the political parliamentary regime in Romania as dualistic. Without coming into conflict with the Parliament or the Government, as the powers of the President of Romania and those of these public authorities are not overlapping but complementary, the President of Romania, mainly in exercising his mediation function, has an important role in the political life of the country. It is on the basis of this role that certain political practices developed, such as consultations of the Head of State with the political parties, intervention by the President for the resolution of some labour conflicts of a national character, etc. Without ruling the country directly, the President participates in its governance through the influence he exerts, particularly upon the executive. However, Romania has a parliamentary regime and therefore it is Parliament that has the supreme role within the cooperation relationships among the public authorities, in accordance with the principle of separation of powers within the State. As has been shown, the control Parliament exerts upon the executive is related to its relationships not only with the Government because of the parliamentary origin thereof but also with the President of Romania, since the exercise of certain powers by the President depends on approval by the Parliament and he is responsible before Parliament for high treason or grave acts infringing upon constitutional provisions.

61. The political parties play an essential role within this political regime. As provided by Article 8 paragraph 2 of the Constitution, political parties may be constituted and pursue their activities in accordance with the law, and they contribute to the definition and expression of the political will of the citizens. To this end, in their capacity as intermediaries between the State and society, the parties are obliged to observe the national sovereignty, the territorial integrity, the legal order and the principles of democracy. Accordingly, the political parties which, by their aims or activity, militate against political pluralism, the principle of the rule of law, or against the sovereignty, integrity or independence of Romania shall be unconstitutional. This rule, contained in Article 40 (former Article 37 in the text of 1991) paragraph 2, should be corroborated with Article 146 paragraph (k), according to which the competence to decide on the unconstitutionality of a political party lies with the Constitutional Court.

Political parties are those entities that concentrate and channel the political aspirations of their militants, adherents and supporters, as well as the latent, diffuse and often contradicting opinions within the society, reflecting the qualitative synthesis thereof, with the aim of conquering, preserving or influencing power by means of a strategy whose main objective is winning the elections. In order to fulfil their purpose, they have to be sustainable political structures, having the nature of an organization, whose purpose is to fulfil an explicit political programme, particularly their electoral platforms.

After the collapse of the communist regime in December 1989, an extremely large number of political parties emerged; however, not all of them are characterized by the features described above. Some of the political parties have regrouped in the meantime. Most lost their proper role, while others merged or established alliances. Then the alliances split again into individual parties, which regrouped once more into larger parties. The multi-party system has therefore been evolving from excessive fragmentation to a functional political pluralism.

62. The overthrow of the communist dictatorship resulted in the emergence of many interest groups, which exerted their influence upon the political and the State's power with the aim of defending their specific interests. Established on the basis of the right to association, some of them also had a political nature, as they militate for objectives whose general nature overlaps the objectives of the political parties, as was the case, for instance, with Alianţa Civică (the Civic Alliance) or Asociaţia Foştilor Deţinuţi Politici (the Association of Former Political Detainees). Others promote exclusively moral interests, such as the leagues for the defence of human rights, the associations of the handicapped, those for the protection of minorities, etc., or certain cultural, religious interests. Certain pressure groups mainly pursue the defence of certain material interests. Within this category, an extremely important role is held by the trade unions, which also enjoy a constitutional protection. Thus, Article 9 of the Constitution provides that trade unions, employers' associations, and vocational associations shall be established and shall carry out their activity according to their statutes, according to the law. They shall contribute to the protection of rights and the promotion of their members' vocational, economic, and social interests.

It has to be pointed out that the text of Article 9 in the Constitution of 1991 only referred to trade unions. The revised text of 2003 added the employers' associations and the vocational associations. In society, pluralism involves not only the role of political parties, provided for under Article 8, but also the role of civil society, particularly that of its main associative forms, which are the unions, the employers' associations and the other associative forms. The express mentioning of employers' associations in the revised text was meant to indicate their important role in the economic and social development of the country.

In the system of constitutional democracy, the role of these forms of association is to defend the rights and promote the professional, economic and social interests of the members of trade unions, employers' or other associations.

The Constitution also lays down the main instruments of the unions' actions – the collective labour contract and the strike – while Law No. 53/2003, republished (the Labour Code), updated and modified several times, more recently by Law No. 367/2022,[71] which also establishes the rules for the organization and functioning thereof, including those referring to the freedom of the trade unions and the provision that they should be independent of the State bodies and the political parties and, at the same time, that they should not perform an activity characteristic of a political party, land by Law No. 283/13.11.2024[72] that reffers to The Ministry of Labour and Social Solidarity, which offers information on the amount of the minimum income, on procedures regarding recourse to labour authorities, and so on.

63. Besides trade unions and employers' associations, there are also other pressure groups pursuing a material objective, some of which have an ever greater influence, such as the consumers' organizations. Some pressure groups have an ad hoc nature, pursuing promotion of a certain initiative. Generally, the developments in this field present great variety and progress extremely rapidly, resulting in a permanently developing network of relationships with the State bodies, mainly the Government, which sometimes are formalized as in the Commission Trade Unions –

71. Published in the Monitorul Oficial, Part I, No. 1238/22.12.2022.
72. Published in The Monitorul Oficial, Part I, No. 1139/14.11.2024.

Government, and also with the political parties which exert an increasing influence upon some of these pressure groups or are supported by them.

A special role is held by the organizations of persons belonging to national minorities. These have an autonomous political role, while at the same time, they act as pressure groups. As a result, they are entitled to a Deputy's seat, which they obtain by designation in case they obtained a sufficient number of votes to claim the right to representation, but not enough to win a full seat in the elections.

Chapter 2. The President of Romania

64. Article 80 paragraph 1 of the Constitution stipulates that the President of Romania represents the Romanian State and safeguards the national independence, unity and territorial integrity. This principle defines the President of Romania as the Head of State.

There are two points of view from which this public authority can be dealt with: an organic point of view, that is, his election, status, constitutional power and competence; and a functional point of view, that is, the exercise of his powers under normal and exceptional circumstances.

As far as the election is concerned, Article 81[73] paragraph 1 of the Constitution provides that the President of Romania shall be elected by universal, equal, direct, secret and free suffrage. Universal, direct suffrage is meant to provide the representativeness, prestige and authority needed for the fulfilment of the role and constitutional powers attributed to the President of Romania. Besides the general conditions for nomination, similar to those for Senators, the candidate in presidential elections shall also meet two special requirements. The first results from the provision of Article 81 paragraph 4 of the Constitution which prohibits any person from holding the office of President of Romania for more than two mandates, whether consecutive or separated by a lapse of time; what is essential is that the person holding the office of President is not able to create an excessive influence by accumulation of a great number of mandates. In addition to this negative requirement, a second requirement, this time a positive one, is provided by the Electoral Act: for the nomination of a person to be registered, it should be supported by at least 100,000 electors. This rule aims to avoid the demagogy of non-representative candidates.

65. The rules governing the presidential elections are similar to those regarding the organization and running of the general elections. The difference lies in that the vote should be given to only one person and, though organized in the constituencies for parliamentary elections, the entire country constitutes a single constituency. In case no candidate obtains the absolute majority of the votes given by the electors registered in the electoral lists in the first ballot, a second ballot shall be organized and the candidate with the largest number of votes shall be declared the winner. However, the second ballot takes place only between the two candidates who gained the largest number of votes in the first ballot. The electoral competition between the first two candidates after the first ballot necessarily polarizes the political dispute and the electors' preferences. These rules are meant to provide the most significant legitimacy to the elected person.

Thus, the Constitutional Court, in its capacity as electoral judge, watches over the observance of the procedure for the election of the President of Romania and confirms the ballot returns (Article 146 paragraph (f) of the Constitution). To this end, according to the electoral law, the Court rules on all challenges emerging during the

73. *See* Law No. 370/2004, on the election of the President of Romania, amended and supplemented by GEO No. 64/2019, published in the Monitorul Oficial, Part I, No. 746/12.9.2019.

elections, asserts the results of the elections after centralization thereof by the Central Electoral Bureau or, as the case may be, the results of the second ballot, and, at the same time, validates the mandate of the elected person.

According to the procedure, first, the validation document is presented to the Chambers of Parliament in joint session. Then the President shall take, before the Chambers, the oath provided by Article 82 paragraph 2 of the Constitution. Starting with the oath-taking date, the President shall exercise his office, while the mandate of the previous President shall cease on that same date.

There is no constitutional provision related to the chronology of the two types of elections. Presidential elections may take place at the same time as the general elections or on a different date. Since the revised text of 2003 modified the President's term of office from four years to five years (Article 83 in both Constitutions), while Parliament's mandate remained unchanged (four years), it is more likely that presidential elections should take place on a different date than the general elections. Anyway, in case they are simultaneous, the President of Romania is the first public authority to be constituted as part of the executive, as a result of the suffrage that took place. In case they are not simultaneous, this problem does not arise since the Government has a parliamentary origin. At present, the political practice resulting from the previous elections is that of simultaneous elections.

66. As was said before, according to the revised text of the Constitution of 2003, the President's term of office is five years. It may be extended in case of war or catastrophe. This rule, provided for by Article 83 paragraph 3 of the Constitution, is similar to that provided for by Article 63 paragraph 1, referring to the Chambers of Parliament.

The similarity between the President's and the Parliament's is found not only as far as the prolongation of terms of office are concerned but also in terms of their prorogation, as provided for by the law: the President's term of office lasts until the newly elected President starts exercising mandate, and the Parliament's mandate lasts until the new Parliament legally meets in joint session. This rule is meant to provide continuity of the presidential and parliamentary functions.

One more similarity between the status of the President of Romania and the status of the Parliament is the independence of opinions. According to Article 84 paragraph 2, the immunity of Parliament Members as regards their expressed opinions shall also apply to the President of Romania. However, as far as inviolability of office is concerned, it has an absolute character in the case of the President, whereas parliamentary immunity may be removed by the Chamber to which the Parliament Member belongs. Nevertheless, there is an exception to this rule: the Chambers of Parliament may decide in joint session for the impeachment of the President of Romania for high treason, through a vote of at least two-thirds of the total number of Parliament Members (Article 96 in the Constitution of 2003). Under such circumstances, the High Court of Cassation and Justice has the competence to rule. It is the only case in which a sitting President can be prosecuted. Of course, presidential immunity – just like the parliamentary one, as a matter of fact – only protects the President while he is in office and, therefore, it is no impediment to judicial responsibility of the person who held the office before. Therefore, presidential immunity is absolute – with the exception mentioned above – but not permanent, unlike immunity for expressed opinions, which is not only absolute but also permanent.

67. The Constitution provides for a number of incompatibilities related to the office of President of Romania. They are specific and tougher than the incompatibilities related to the office of Parliament Member. The most important difference is that contained in Article 84 paragraph 1, according to which, during his term of office, the President of Romania may not be a member of any political party. This means that even though the nominations in the presidential elections are proposed by political parties – which, however, do not necessarily imply that a candidate be a member of the party that supported his nomination – the candidate who is elected President can no longer be member of any political party. The supreme office of the State, that is the office of the President of Romania, is contrary to the leading and discipline of a political party. Since the President of the country is the President of all citizens, he cannot be politically subordinated to a segment represented by a political party. The merging of party leadership and State leadership, which characterized Ceauşescu's dictatorship during the period of communist totalitarianism, proved its deeply vicious and dangerous nature. From this point of view, the supreme magistracy within the State exercised by the President of Romania is similar – though for other reasons – to that of judges, who also cannot be politically enrolled to prevent any influence that may prejudice their impartiality. As a matter of fact, non-involvement of the President with the political competition of parties is a condition for performing his role of mediator between the State authorities as well as between the State and society, as required by Article 80 paragraph 2 of the Constitution.

The President of Romania cannot hold any other public or private office, the only exception being that provided under Article 92 paragraph 1 of the Constitution, according to which he is also the President of the Supreme Council of National Defence. It is an exigency more rigid than with any other public office or dignity, justified by the constitutional position of the President.

The presidential immunities and incompatibilities that have been mentioned above are aimed at establishing a specific judicial regime for the protection of the presidential office, with the end of preventing any influence, wherever it may come from, that could impair performance of the President in his functions. Such influences, by their very nature, are contrary to the constitutional equidistant position of the President of Romania.

68. Article 95 of the Constitution provides that the President of Romania may be suspended from office by the Chamber of Deputies and the Senate in joint session, in case he committed grave acts infringing upon constitutional provisions. The proposal for suspension can be initiated by at least a third of the number of Parliament Members. Therefore, the initiative for such a measure can be taken only by Parliament. In order to be submitted for debate, the proposal shall be the topic of an investigation by the Parliament and then, according to Article 95 paragraph 1 and Article 146 paragraph (h) of the Constitution, be submitted for an advisory opinion to the Constitutional Court. The measure of suspension can be adopted upon the vote of the majority of Parliament Members expressed in a joint session of the two Chambers.

The President's suspension from office has the following effects: the interim of office shall start and so does the term of thirty days provided for by Article 95 paragraph 3 of the Constitution, within which a referendum shall be organized for the President's deposition. This final solution is the consequence of a principle of symmetry: since the President was elected by the voters, he can only be removed from office as a result of their will. Throughout the entire procedure of suspension, either before the Parliament or before the Constitutional Court, the President has the possibility to express his viewpoints for his defence, for as early as initiation of the procedure, he shall be notified about the proposal of suspension. At the same time, he may also voice his opinions within the framework of the referendum organized to remove him from office.

Parliament's ability to bring a charge of high treason against the President of Romania or to suspend him from office for serious infringement upon constitutional provisions proves that the essential aspects of the exercise of the presidential office are controlled by Parliament. Parliamentary control over the presidential office is related to other aspects too. These refer to the way the President exercises certain powers, which we shall not deal with herein. What we are interested in relation to the President's status are the elements that may lead to his suspension, in the juridical sense of the term, either criminal, or by suspension of the exercise of his office. In all these cases, the Parliament's decision is not a final one. The Parliament may substitute neither the juridical power, in case of the high treason impeachment, nor the electorate, in case of a charge of serious infringement upon constitutional provisions. Therefore, the peculiarity of the parliamentary control lies in that it triggers the procedures for the President's dismissal, either by a conviction decision or through the referendum organized after his suspension from office. Thus, the decision of Parliament is subject to control, which may be either juridical and exercised by the High Court of Cassation and Justice in case of the high treason impeachment or by the electorate in the case of suspension from office. This possibility of refutation by the judiciary or by the electorate constitutes an important guarantee against abusive exercise of this constitutional power, exclusively inspired by political reasons.

69. The President's dismissal (by either of the two cases presented above) induces vacancy of the office of the President of Romania. These are the only ways through which vacancy of office can be the result of parliamentary initiative, though the actual dismissal of the President is given by the juridical power – according to Article 96, paragraph 3 of the Constitution, the President shall be removed from office de jure on the date the Court sentence becomes final – or by the electorate within the framework of the referendum organized after his suspension from office. Vacancy of office may also result from resignation – therefore, at the President's initiative – or permanent inability to discharge his powers and duties, or death – therefore, under objective circumstances.

Whatever the case may be, as Article 146 paragraph (g) of the Constitution provides, existence of the circumstances which justify the interim of office shall be ascertained by the Constitutional Court which has the obligation to notify the Parliament and the Government of its resolution. Therefore, in the case of a conviction decision, the Court shall be bound to ascertain its final nature. In the case of a referendum, the approval of the dismissal measure must be notified – according to Article 146 paragraph (i) of the Constitution, the Court shall safeguard the observance of the procedure for the organization and holding of a referendum, whatever its nature, constitutional, consultative or for the President's dismissal. In the case of inability to discharge his powers and duties, the Court must ascertain not only that the impediment is absolute but also that it is permanent.

70. If vacancy of office occurs, then there will be an interim office. According to Article 98 paragraph 1 of the Constitution, it shall also occur in case the President is suspended from office or temporarily incapable of exercising his powers.

Under such circumstances (vacancy of office), according to Article 97 paragraph 2 of the Constitution, the Government is bound to organize elections for a new President, within three months at the most. In the case of suspension or temporary incapacity, the President shall resume the exercise of his mandate when the circumstances justifying the interim come to an end. Therefore, in case of vacancy of office, the interim is the result of cessation of the President's mandate other than through election of a new President, while in the other situations, it is the result of the de jure or de facto inability of the President to exercise his mandate.

The conditions justifying the interim of office shall be in all cases ascertained by the Constitutional Court, which thus provides the juridical act by which the office of President, during the interim period, shall be exercised by the President of the Senate or the President of the Chamber of Deputies, in this order. The interim President has the same status as the elected President and exercises the same powers, with certain exceptions, however, to which we shall refer when presenting the President's constitutional competence.

71. As far as the powers of the President of Romania are concerned, some of the President's constitutional powers traditionally belong to the Head of State, while others are specific to the development of this office in the present constitutional context of the country.

The category of *traditional powers* could be further divided into the following groups of powers, as provided by the Constitution:

1. Prevailingly political powers: these include designation of the candidate for the office of Prime Minister and appointment of the Government on the basis of the vote of confidence of the Parliament (Article 85 paragraph 1 and Article 103 paragraph 1); dismissal and appointment of the Ministers, on proposal by the Prime Minister, in case of a Government reshuffle (Article 85 paragraph 2); if, through the reshuffle proposal, the political structure or composition of

the Government is changed (Article 85, paragraph 3);[74] as well as appointment of interim Ministers, also on proposal by the Prime Minister (Article 107); however, the President of Romania cannot dismiss the Prime Minister (Article 107 paragraph 2); presiding over the Government's meetings which the President attends and consultation with the Government about urgent, extremely important matters (Articles 86 and 87); addressing Parliament on the main political issues of the nation (Article 88); dissolution of Parliament (Article 89); request for re-examination of a law prior to promulgation; presidential suspending veto (Article 77 paragraph 2).

2. Prevailingly executive powers: this category includes promulgation of laws (Article 77 paragraph 1), institution of the state of siege or emergency (Article 93), triggering of criminal prosecution against members of the Government for offences committed in the exercise of their office, suspension from office of those against whom criminal prosecution has been requested (Article 108), designation for certain public offices, conferring decorations and titles of honour (Article 94).
3. Powers in the field of foreign policy: these include representation of the Romanian State in international relations (Article 80 paragraph 1), conclusion of international treaties in the name of Romania and submission thereof to Parliament for ratification, accreditation and recall of diplomatic envoys, setting up, closing down or change in rank of diplomatic missions as well as reception of diplomatic envoys of other States (Article 91).
4. Powers in the military field: the President of Romania is guarantor of the national independence, of the country's unity and territorial integrity (Article 80 paragraph 1) on the basis of which he is the Commander-in-Chief of the Armed Forces and the President of the Supreme Council of National Defence; also, the President of Romania may declare, upon prior approval by Parliament and, in exceptional cases, on subsequent approval thereof, partial or general mobilization of the Armed Forces and he has the competence to take the necessary measures for the repelling of aggression against the country, on undelayed notification of the Parliament (Article 92).
5. Powers in relation to the Constitution: this category includes the President's obligation to safeguard the observance of the Constitution and the proper functioning of the public authorities (Article 80 paragraph 2) and his right to initiative for revision of the Constitution, on proposal by the Government (Article 150 paragraph 1).
6. Powers in the judicial field: the right to grant individual pardon (Article 94 paragraph (d)) and appointment to office of judges and prosecutors, except for those on probation, on proposal by the Superior Council of Magistracy.

Besides the traditional powers, the Constitution also confers the President of Romania *new competencies.* The most important power in this category is the function of mediating between the powers in the State, as well as between the State and

74. Decision No. 98/7.2.2008 of the Constitutional Court, published within the Monitorul Oficial, Part I, No. 22/7.2.2008; Decision No. 779/17.6.2011 regarding the Draft Law for Constitutional Revision, published in the Monitorul Oficial, Part I, No. 440/23.6.2011.

society. On the basis of this function, provided for by Article 80 paragraph 2 of the Constitution, the President of Romania exercises a 'moral' magistracy, that involves his authority, influence and persuasive force, especially with a view to unlocking the machinery and formulae of compromise necessary for the avoidance and, as the case may be, settlement of conflicts between public authorities or between the latter and segments of the civil society such as trade unions, employers' associations, religious, ethnic and other organizations.

This category also includes the President's right to call the people, after consultation with the Parliament, to express its will as to issues of national interest by means of a referendum (Article 90).

The President has the right to ask the Constitutional Court, according to Article 146 paragraph (a) of the Constitution, to rule as to the constitutionality of a law prior to promulgation, and the right to appoint three of the Constitutional Court's judges (Article 140 paragraph 2).

In principle, the President of Romania exercises a power that is shared either with the Government, since his acts shall be countersigned by the Prime Minister, the Government thus assuming its responsibility for those acts, or with Parliament, in case the issued act shall be submitted for approval by Parliament, or with another public authority. Shared powers are those in the fields of foreign policy and defence, the institution of the state of siege or emergency, the granting of decorations and titles of honour, the granting of the ranks of marshal, general or admiral, and the granting of individual pardon: according to Article 100 paragraph 2 of the Constitution, the acts issued by the President can only be issued if countersigned by the Prime Minister. Similarly, a Government reshuffle or appointment of an interim Minister shall be performed on proposal of the Prime Minister. The initiative of revision of the Constitution is exercised on proposal by the Government. As regards institution of the state of siege or emergency, these shall be submitted to Parliament for prior approval or, in exceptional cases, later approval. The appointment of judges is done on proposal by the Superior Council of Magistracy. Therefore, shared competence is the rule.

72. Nevertheless, the President also has powers whose exercise depends exclusively on his will. These are, among others: the appointment of the candidate for the office of Prime Minister (who afterwards applies to Parliament for the vote of confidence); the messages addressed to Parliament; the request for re-examination of a law prior to promulgation – the presidential suspending veto; the dissolution of Parliament; consultation of the people by means of a referendum; consultation of the Government or participation in the latter's meetings when such problems as foreign policy, national defence or public order are debated; appointment of three judges to the Constitutional Court.

73. On the contrary, there are certain powers (actually duties) which the President cannot refuse. Thus, he is bound to appoint the Government on the basis of the vote of confidence granted by Parliament, and to promulgate a law in case the objection of unconstitutionality was rejected by Parliament.

74. As far as the powers of the interim President are concerned, the latter has the constitutional status of the elected President and has the same powers as the President of Romania except for those of addressing messages to Parliament, of dissolving Parliament and of consulting the people by means of a referendum (Article 98 paragraph 2 of the Constitution).

Article 100 of the Constitution provides that, in the exercise of his powers, the President of Romania shall issue decrees that are only valid if published in the *Monitorul Oficial of Romania.*

As far as the President of Romania's exercise of the office is concerned, two aspects are essential: on the one hand, his relationship with the Government in the framework of the executive power and, on the other hand, his relationship with Parliament.

75. The President's direct election by the people, through universal suffrage, gives his legitimacy. However, the Government is of parliamentary origin, since it is appointed by the President on the basis of the vote of confidence granted by Parliament and is politically responsible only before the latter. For this reason, the relationship between the two public authorities within the executive – the President of Romania and the Government – is a relationship of cooperation. The Government participates in the exercise of the President of Romania's competencies shared with the Prime Minister, since the countersigning of the presidential acts or, as the case may be, their achievement only on proposal by the Prime Minister, involves, as a result of governmental solidarity, the responsibility of the entire Government. There are also other competencies exercised by the President of Romania on initiative by the Government, such as the conclusion of international treaties which, according to Article 91 paragraph 1 of the Constitution, are negotiated by the Government; and the initiative for revision of the Constitution, which is taken by the President on proposal by the Government. The initiative of cooperation may also lie with the President, such as when the members of the Government are consulted, when the President participates in the Government's meetings dealing with foreign policy issues, when national defence or public order are at stake, etc.

As a rule, the effectiveness of the executive's action depends a great deal on the President. He is not involved in the definition of the governmental programme approved by Parliament when the vote of confidence is granted. His political independence is also based on the fact that, as has been shown, the President cannot be a member of a political party. This makes it easier for him to take action. His constitutional position, equidistant in relation to the political forces represented in the Government and in Parliament, allows him to cooperate with the Government, irrespective of its political orientation. Also, sharing of the competencies between the President and the Government is achieved from different positions. The President acts in his capacity as guarantor of the national independence and of the country's territorial unity and integrity, as mediator between the powers within the State and between the State and society, and as safeguard for the observance of the Constitution and the proper functioning of the public authorities (Article 80 of the Constitution). The Government acts in its capacity as the authority ensuring the performance of the domestic and foreign policy of the country, according to its programme of governance, and as the general manager of the public administration

(Article 102 of the Constitution). These two roles are complementary but do not overlap, and, while they can empower each other, they cannot exclude each other. For this reason, each of the two authorities defining the dualism of the executive's structure can perform its role, thus defining the executive's place in the framework of the political regime.

76. The relationship between Parliament and the President can be seen in terms of two features. The fact that the President is not responsible before Parliament – which is, however, attenuated by the latter's possibility to prosecute the President for high treason or suspend him from office for serious infringement upon the Constitution – is a logical consequence of his election by the people and provides him with an independent position. However, Parliament has the role of a censor of the President's most important acts, performed by the latter on the basis of his constitutional competencies.

Here are some examples of the President's independence in his relationship with Parliament: the presidential messages by means of which the President presents the Chambers with his opinion on the main political problems of the nation, thus triggering debates and a dialogue; the suspending veto the President can attach to a law prior to promulgation while requesting re-examination of the law; the dissolution of Parliament after consultations with the Presidents of the two Chambers and the leaders of the parliamentary groups, in case of a long-term governmental crisis (at least sixty days) or a deadlock (at least two failed attempts to form a new Government); the right to initiation of a consultative referendum so that the people be able to express their will in relation to a problem of national interest, after consultations with Parliament.

Examples illustrating Parliament's controlling role are: the President's obligation to apply to Parliament for prior approval for the mobilization of the Armed Forces, institution of the state of siege or emergency or, under exceptional circumstances, for later approval which must be requested within five days at the utmost since the taking of such measures; and the President's obligation to notify Parliament by means of a message about the measures taken for the repel of an aggression, in which case the latter shall be convened within twenty-four hours at the utmost after the beginning of the aggression.

77. Even though the President's relationship with the Government and with Parliament is essential for the definition of the presidential function, it is also important to study his relationships with other public authorities. In this respect, mention should be made of: intimation by the President of the Constitutional Court for the resolution of an objection of unconstitutionally prior to promulgation of a law; appointment of judges on proposal by the Superior Council of Magistracy, etc. It is also worth mentioning the President's role as an arbiter in mediating the relationships between the State and society, which implies his involvement, particularly for the attenuation and settlement of conflict situations in any field, by means of dialogue, political negotiations, and formulae of compromise, for the avoidance of forms of violent confrontation. It is an extremely important role, particularly in a period of transition with all the turmoil it involves.

The obvious conclusion to the preceding discussion on the President of Romania is that his constitutional position is that of a public authority directly invested by the people, thus enjoying the legitimacy of a mandated representative of the entire electorate, equidistant and outside the political competition of the political parties. In his capacity as Head of State, he represents the country and is the guarantor of national independence and of the country's territorial unity and integrity. He monitors the observance of the Constitution and the proper functioning of public authorities and exercises the function of mediator between the powers within the State and between the State and society.

Chapter 3. Parliament of Romania

78. Article 61 paragraph 1 of the Constitution gives the definition of Parliament: it is the people's supreme representative body and the country's unique legislative authority. This synthetic definition of Parliament's constitutional status basically provides its precedence within the political regime and thus the parliamentary character of this regime.

In its capacity as the people's supreme representative body, Parliament's legitimacy and structure are the direct result of national sovereignty expressed through the will of the electorate at the polls. Parliament's origin is elective and its entire activity is placed under elective control. Likewise, as an exponent of the people's political interests, Parliament cannot be subordinated to any private, local, or group interests that would come into conflict with those of the whole society. This is mainly expressed through Parliament's legislative function and through its function of control over all other public authorities, particularly the executive – the President of Romania and the Government.

In the framework of the constitutional regime, Parliament's legislative function is traditional. Parliament is the only holder of the legislative power, therefore, the only authority invested with the prerogative to lay down the general will in the form of laws. This also implies the right to grant the Government the power to regulate certain matters on the basis of legislative delegation, and at the same time, characterizes the special relationship between Parliament and the President of Romania in relation to the promulgation of laws.

The following analysis will focus on the structure of Parliament, the status of Parliament Members, Parliament's organization and its functions.

79. As Article 61 paragraph 2 of the Constitution stipulates, Parliament consists of the Chamber of Deputies and the Senate.[75] The dualism of Parliament's structure corresponds to the bicephalous structure of the executive, represented by the President of Romania and the Government. It is not only the expression of a tradition (Parliament had a two-Chamber structure during the democratic inter-war period) but also of an institutional necessity, for the optimization of the legislative process, especially with a view to ensuring the quality of the law-making and to avoid the concentration of power in a one-Chamber Parliament, as with communist totalitarianism.

Characteristic of the Romanian Parliament is that the two Chambers hold an equal position. Since they are directly elected by the people by universal suffrage, they have an equal legitimacy, which also justifies the fact that their prerogatives are not different. Nevertheless, there are some differences which are important but do not affect the equal position of the Chambers. As shown before, both The Chamber of Deputies and the Senate can be the decisional chamber, according to the

75. *See also* the following: The Regulations of the Chamber of Deputies, the consolidated version on 30 Jan. 2023. The Regulations of the Senate approved on 24 Oct. 2005, republished in the Monitorul Oficial, Part I, No. 1176/8.12.2022.

nature of the law and the order of notification, still the Senate is more often the decisional chamber. Moreover, there are fewer Senators than Deputies, so that the parties' political representation in the Senate is also narrower; the minimum age for Senators is 33 (35 in the text of 1991), unlike the case of the President of Romania, for whom the minimum age is 35, while for Deputies it is 23, as in the bodies of local autonomy (Article 37 of the Constitution); and it is the Senate and the Chamber of Deputies that appoint, in joint session, the People's Advocate Institution (Article 58 correlated with Article 65, paragraph 2, letter (i) of the Constitution).

To avoid an institutional blocking, which, owing to the Chambers' equal position, could occur in case there was an irreconcilable disagreement between the two Chambers, the Chambers are to meet in joint session. Joint sessions are also required for votes of confidence and no confidence in the Government, suspension from office of the President of Romania, the adoption of the State budget and the State social security budget, the declaration of the state of war, the suspension or ending of military hostilities, the examination of the reports of the Supreme Council of National Defence and of the Court of Audit, etc. According to Article 65 paragraph 1 of the Constitution, the joint session is a working method of the Chambers and not a parliamentary body. It occurs when the Chambers are to debate upon an urgent problem of national interest, which concerns the Parliament as a whole and not just each particular Chamber.

80. Parliament is elected through universal, equal, direct, secret and free suffrage, in accordance with the electoral law (Article 62 paragraph 1). The only exception is that of the Deputy mandate obtained through designation by the organizations of citizens belonging to national minorities that did not receive the number of votes needed to be represented in Parliament. According to Article 62 paragraph 2 of the Constitution, these organizations are entitled to one Deputy seat, for which, however, it is necessary that they should have obtained a sufficient number of votes to claim representativeness.

As Article 63 of the Constitution provides, the term of office is four years, and it may be extended by an organic law in case of war or catastrophe. Also, according to paragraph 4 of the same Article, in order to ensure the continuity of parliamentary activity, the mandate of the Chambers shall be extended until the new Parliament, resulting from the general elections, legally meets. For the periods when the Chambers' term of office is extended, Parliament's legislative competence is affected: it cannot review the Constitution and cannot pass, modify or abrogate organic laws.

81. The new Parliament shall legally meet on the date when the majority of the mandates in each Chamber are validated. The rule takes into account the fact that general elections shall take place within three months at the most since expiry of the four-year mandate or since Parliament's dissolution and that the newly elected Parliament shall be convened by the President of Romania within twenty days at the most after the elections. The Chambers' four-year term of office may be interrupted through Parliament's dissolution by the President of Romania, according to Article 89 of the Constitution, if no vote of confidence has been obtained for a Government within sixty days after the first request was made, and only after rejection of at least two requests for investiture of a Government. In a year, Parliament can be dissolved only once. It cannot be dissolved during the last six months of the term of office of the President of Romania, nor can it be dissolved during a state of siege or emergency.

In case the Chambers' term of office ceases, then the terms of office of Deputies and Senators shall also collectively cease. Article 70 paragraph 2 of the Constitution states that the capacity as Deputy or Senator shall cease on the day that the newly elected Chambers legally meet. The term of office of Parliament Members may also cease in case of resignation, disenfranchisement, incompatibility, or death. Under such circumstances, the vacant seat shall be occupied by the next candidate on the electoral list in question, as all non-elected persons on that list have the capacity of substitutes, provided that they have maintained their political adherence. If there is no candidate left, who meets the requirements, on the list, by-elections will be held for the vacant seat.

82. Parliament Members shall enjoy immunity in the exercise of their mandate; they cannot be held judicially responsible for the votes or political opinions they express, and cannot be retained, arrested, searched, or sued for criminal or minor offences without approval by the Chamber they belong to. In case of a flagrant offence, a Parliament Member may be retained or searched, but the Chamber he belongs to shall be notified in order to rule on the suspension of immunity. In all cases, the competence to give judgment lies with the High Court of Cassation and Justice.

In relation to incompatibilities, the Constitution provides in its Article 71 that no one may be a Deputy and a Senator at the same time; also, that the capacity as a Deputy or Senator is incompatible with the exercise of any public office in authority, with the exception of Government membership, while other incompatibilities shall be established by organic law.

In terms of protection of the parliamentary mandate, in addition to the immunities provided under Article 72, it is also given by the monthly pay and the meeting pay, as well as the other legal rights – free transportation and accommodation, daily travelling allowance, territorial office, etc.

83. Article 61 of the Constitution stipulates the principle according to which Parliament's Chambers are organized, namely, parliamentary autonomy. Based on this principle, enshrined by, each Chamber has its own political composition, resulting from its organization into parliamentary groups, its own managing and working bodies – standing parliamentary commissions, inquiry and special commissions, groups of friendship with various countries – and its own budget. The organization of the Chambers complies with their own organization and functioning statutes. Besides the statute of each particular Chamber, there is a statute for the joint sessions, which only refers to the working methods of the Chambers in joint sessions.

The criterion according to which parliamentary groups are organized is political affinity. They have a special importance not only for the parliamentary activity but also for the establishment of Parliament's managing and working bodies – the

Standing Bureau and the parliamentary commissions – whose composition shall reflect the political configuration of each Chamber.

84. Each Chamber establishes the number and the powers of its parliamentary commissions. The Chambers may also establish joint commissions, such as the Commission for the control over the Romanian Information Service.

There are two types of commissions. Thus, the standing commissions prepare the materials that are to be debated in plenary sessions. To this end, they pass advisory opinions on the bills and on the legislative proposals presented. At the same time, on demand of the Plenum of the Chamber, they make inquiries in their professional field. If the material is to be debated upon in joint sessions, the commissions of the two Chambers shall work together.

The inquiry or special commissions are ad hoc, and they have to perform a specific task assigned by the Chamber: the conduct of a parliamentary inquiry, the editing of a legislative proposal, the passing of an advisory opinion upon a bill, etc.

On proposal by the parliamentary groups, the President, the Standing Bureau and each commission's members are elected. The President of the Chamber and the parliamentary commissions are established for the entire term of office. The Standing Bureaus are elected at the beginning of each ordinary session. The Chamber may revoke the President or a Standing Bureau member, while the parliamentary groups may withdraw the support granted to a parliamentary commission member, in which case a new election takes place.

85. Traditionally, parliamentary Chambers work in sessions. Ordinary sessions take place twice a year: from February to the end of June, and from September to the end of December. Extraordinary sessions are convened by the Presidents of the Chambers, on request by the President of Romania, by the Standing Bureau of each Chamber, or by at least a third of the total number of Deputies or Senators. Extraordinary sessions may also be de jure, as is the case when the state of emergency is decreed, when the Government submits an urgent ordinance for parliamentary approval, or when an armed aggression against the country is triggered.

86. Parliament can be defined as a deliberating authority which debates on the nation's political problems. While such a definition refers to the whole of the functions performed by Parliament, the following discussion is devoted to three essential aspects of the parliamentary activity: *the legislative procedure*, *the control procedure* and *the procedure for the establishment of certain State bodies*. There are different opinions concerning Parliament's functions, as its activity is wider and more complex than the rigidity of any theoretical schemes, even from a functional point of view. In this respect, one could mention the debates of a purely political character, the Chambers' external activity, the commemorative meetings, etc., which obviously do not belong within the previously mentioned typology. Nevertheless, we have chosen these three functions – the legislative function, the control one, and the appointing one – as they are the most characteristic of the definition of Parliament's constitutional role and position within the political regime and because they represent the largest amount of activity of Parliament's Chambers.

87. Speaking about Parliament's legislative function, Article 61 paragraph 1 of the Constitution stipulates that Parliament is the sole legislative authority of the State. This capacity is expressed by Parliament's legislative competence.[76]

In spite of the fact that Parliament is the only legislative authority, its legislative competence is nevertheless shared, in certain respects, with the Government and the President of Romania. Thus, the Government holds the exclusive right to elaborate the State budget and the State social security budget, while the President of Romania, by demanding the reconsideration of a law, exercises a right of suspending veto, resulting in a new debate on some aspects of the adopted law prior to promulgation. These powers of the Government and the President do not conflict with Parliament's capacity as the country's unique legislative authority, since they do not at all affect the fact that a law may be passed by Parliament only as an expression of its sovereign will.

Parliament's legislative competence is also shared, to a certain extent, with the jurisdiction of the Constitutional Court, since a decision by which the Court finds a law or a legal provision unconstitutional prior to promulgation shall be submitted for debate to Parliament's Chambers. In case both Chambers pass the law in its initial form by a majority of two-thirds, the objection of unconstitutionality is rejected and promulgation becomes compulsory. The debate shall only deal with the constitutional character of the law. Nevertheless, the fact that, within these limits, the law is again submitted to the Chambers for debate means that the decision has the effect of a suspension. If the decision is rejected, adoption of the law in its initial form is equal to a constitutional interpretation by Parliament, and then the respective law cannot later become the subject of an objection of unconstitutionality.

As a rule, three stages can be traced down as constitutive elements of the legislative process: the legislative initiative, the legislative procedure, and the promulgation and publication of the law.

88. Since the progress of the legislative process depends upon the typology provided for by Article 73 paragraph 1 of the Constitution, according to which laws are constitutional, organic, or ordinary, *the legislative initiative* varies in terms of this typology. With constitutional laws – i.e., laws for the revision of the Constitution – the initiative lies, according to Article 150 of the Constitution, with the President of Romania on proposal of the Government, by at least one-quarter of the number of Deputies or Senators, or by at least 500,000 citizens with the right to vote. In the latter case, the citizens who initiate the revision of the Constitution must belong to at least half the number of the counties in the country, and in each of the respective counties including the City of Bucharest at least 20,000 signatures must be recorded in support of this initiative. For a revision to be initiated, the proposal shall be endorsed by the Legislative Council and the Constitutional Court. Even though the endorsement is an advisory one, its request is nevertheless compulsory.

According to Article 74 paragraph 1 of the Constitution, in the case of organic or ordinary laws, the legislative initiative lies with the Government, Deputies, Senators, as well as no fewer than 100,000 citizens having the right to vote. The citizens

76. Irina Moroianu Zlătescu, *La function legislative du Parlement en droit comparé* (OTAN, Bruxelles, 1996), pp. 71 and the following.

having the right to legislative initiative must belong to at least one-quarter of the country's counties, while in each of these counties or the city of Bucharest, at least 5,000 signatures should be registered in support of this initiative. However, fiscal issues, issues of an international character, amnesty and pardoning cannot be the citizens' legislative initiatives.

With the exception of constitutional laws, all the other laws are either organic or ordinary.

In their capacity as very important regulations within the legislative system, organic laws are restrictively defined by the Constitution. Their importance comes from the fact that they refer to the main public authorities – the Government, the Supreme Council of National Defence, the People's Advocate Institution, the Court of Audit, the organization of the courts of law, the Legislative Council, etc. – in which respect they represent an extension of the Constitution. They also refer to the major aspects of the country's political and economic system – the electoral regime, the political parties, the referendum, the regime of the state of emergency, the status of public servants, the general regime of property and legacy, labour relations, trade unions and social protection, organization for education, etc.

89. According to the *legislative procedure*, both drafts of law (or bills) – which are governmental initiatives – and legislative proposals – which are Parliament's or citizens' initiatives – shall be endorsed by the Legislative Council, according to Article 79 (paragraph 1) of the Constitution, in order to have a systematized, unified and coordinated legislation. The endorsement is advisory.

Before going any further with the description of the legislative procedure, just a few words about an institution that traditionally plays an extremely important role in the development of this process: the Legislative Council. According to its organic founding law,[77] the role of the Legislative Council is to provide systematization, unification and coordination of the legislation, both prior to the parliamentary legislative procedure and in the course thereof. For this reason, the endorsement by the Legislative Council represents an admissibility condition for the submission of drafts of laws and legislative proposals, as well as, on request by the President of the Chamber, intimated on the merits, for the debates upon the drafts received by a Chamber after they have been passed by the other Chamber, or for the formulated amendments. The Legislative Council shall also endorse the drafts of ordinances or normative decisions prior to being submitted for adoption by the Government. At the same time, on demand by one of Parliament's Chambers, the Legislative Council shall elaborate drafts of Codes or other laws of high complexity and conduct studies on the systematization, unification and coordination of the legislation. On its own initiative, it shall intimate the Standing Bureaus of Parliament's Chambers in case it finds inconsistencies between the legal provisions in effect and the Constitution.

77. Law No. 73/3.11.1993, on establishing the Legislative Council, modified and supplemented by Law No. 509/2004. The latest amendment was on 15.12.2022, by Law No. 343/9.12.2022, published in the Monitorul Oficial, Part I, No. 1191/12.12.2022. In reference to the Legislative Council, *see* Valer Dorneanu, *Consiliul Legislativ la 25 de ani de la reînfiinţare: dovadă vie şi elocventă a utilităţii şi importanţei sale*, in *Buletin de Informare Legislativă* nr. 2 (Editura Monitorul Oficial, Bucureşti, 2021), p. 17.

90. Now, to resume the presentation of the legislative procedure, it is important to point out that adoption of a law consists of two successive stages: the first one starts with the preparation of the plenary working sessions, provides the analysis, the endorsement, and the documentation, and ends as soon as the draft of law or the legislative proposal is put on the agenda; the second one consists in the debates and the vote.

The decisive role in the preparing stage lies with the commission intimated on the merits, whose task is to endorse the draft as a whole, by proposing acceptance or rejection thereof, and to pass motivated opinions about the endorsements by other commissions and the amendments received from Parliament Members, parliamentary groups or the Government.

As was mentioned above, the second stage starts with the discussions in Plenum, which include the debate of principle. The latter is concluded with a vote only if the report by the commission intimated on the merits proposes the rejection of the draft. The discussions in Plenum also include the debate and the vote on each article, as well as the final vote on the law as a whole, as it has been amended during the debates on articles. Either Chamber may be the first to be intimated. This is one consequence of the equality between Parliament's two Chambers. After the law has been passed by one of the Chambers, it shall be sent for debate to the other Chamber. If the second Chamber passes the law without any modification, the law shall be submitted for promulgation not before five days, or two days in case of a rush procedure, during which it shall be made available to Parliament Members, to the Government, and to the High Court of Cassation and Justice so that they will be able to intimate the Constitutional Court with an objection of unconstitutionality. The right to formulate such an objection operates until the date of promulgation. The term of five and two days respectively is meant to prevent a possible inability to exercise this right.

In case the draft of law or the legislative proposal that was passed by the first Chamber to be intimated is rejected by the second Chamber, it shall be sent back to the first Chamber for new debates meant to reach a compromise. A new rejection is final.

It is also possible for the second Chamber to pass the draft in a different form. In this case, a mediating procedure shall follow through a commission where the two Chambers are equally represented. The aim of the commission is to settle the divergences and to adopt a unique form of the draft which both Chambers would pass. If divergences cannot be settled by the mediating commission or the latter's viewpoint is not accepted by the two Chambers, the Chambers shall be convened in joint session to debate upon the divergences, to settle them, and to finally pass the draft.

The legislative procedure can be resumed after a draft law has been passed as a result of the President of Romania's request that the law be reconsidered. In this case, the debate shall be started in the initially first intimated Chamber. At the same time, within the limits that were shown, resuming the procedure is also possible in case the Constitutional Court has decided that the law or certain provisions thereof are unconstitutional.

91. As was mentioned earlier, the final stage of the legislative process consists of the *promulgation* and *publication* of the law. According to Article 77 of the Constitution, the President of Romania is obliged to promulgate the law within twenty days. If he has requested that the law be reconsidered, or a review has been asked for as to its conformity with the Constitution, promulgation shall be made within ten days from receiving the law passed after its reconsideration, or the decision of the Constitutional Court confirming its constitutionality. The term is the same in case the law was received after reconsideration by Parliament following a decision of unconstitutionality by the Constitutional Court.

The task to ensure publication of the law in the *Monitorul Oficial of Romania* lies with the Chamber of Deputies. As specified under Article 78 of the Constitution, a law comes into force on the day of publication or the date provided in its text.

92. It was mentioned earlier that a second and also very important function performed by Parliament is that of *parliamentary control*. This function is exercised not only through the *special control procedures* but also as part of the legislative procedure, of the debates upon the political declarations by the Prime Minister presented in Parliament, and of the debates on presidential messages. In all such circumstances, Parliament Members, in their capacity as censors of governmental activity, oblige the executive to give explanations of its legislative or other policy, be it sector-related or global, and to argue in favour of its position and viewpoints.

For such reasons as length and structure of the presentation, only the special control procedures will be described here. The *questioning procedure*, by which Government members have to explain a certain fact, is one of them; by *interpellations*, Government members are compelled to explain their policy in a certain field of activity; the *parliamentary inquiry* is a means to investigate the activity in a certain sector of social life; by the motion of censure, a general debate upon the Government's policy is triggered with a view to put an end to its mandate through withdrawal by Parliament of the confidence it granted to the Government at the latter's investiture. Questions may be oral or written. Interpellations may generate a debate concluded with the adoption of a motion expressing the position of the Chamber where the interpellation took place in relation to the issue that was the topic of the interpellation. The parliamentary inquiry is always an investigation of a certain problem related either to the executive's activity – which is the general rule – or some other aspect of social activity, such as a highly important event. It may be carried out either by standing commission, provided the topic falls into the respective commission's field of activity, or by an inquiry commission, established to this end. Since it is an ad hoc commission, the activity of a parliamentary inquiry commission ceases once its report has been debated upon. It shall be formed according to the general principle for the formation of parliamentary commissions, under which the reflection of the political structure of the assembly is to be observed. Under all circumstances, the parliamentary inquiry shall be ordered by the Plenum of the assembly and be concluded within the period of time thus established.

93. According to Article 113 paragraph 2 of the Constitution, the motions of censure are collective only and must be initiated by at least one-fourth of the total number of Deputies and Senators. Its purpose is to have a debate on the entire governmental policy, culminating in withdrawal of the confidence granted to the Government. The motion shall be debated upon three days after its presentation in joint session of the Chambers, and shall be passed by the votes of the absolute majority of the Parliament Members. If the motion is passed, the procedure for the investiture of a new Government shall be triggered; if it fails to be passed, the Parliament Members who signed it may not submit another one during the same session, except if the Government assumes political responsibility in a certain matter. In the latter case, the Government, in an attempt to mobilize the majority it relies on, assumes its responsibility regarding a draft of law, a statement or a programme, which it considers essential for its functioning. This procedure is, in fact, a challenge addressed to the Chambers, by which the Government wants to verify the confidence it can rely on. In such a case, unless a motion of censure is registered within three days or if such a motion is rejected, the draft of law shall be considered passed, or, as the case may be, the statement or the programme shall be considered accepted (Article 114 paragraph 3 of the Constitution). Since the motion of censure is provoked by the Government itself, the interdiction regarding the signing thereof by those who had previously during the same session initiated a motion which was rejected shall not apply.

94. There are also more complex control procedures, which have some other purposes in addition to the parliamentary control. Thus, the parliamentary inquiry, particularly when its effect is the engagement of the penal responsibility of a Government member or the impeachment of the President of Romania for high treason or suspension from office of the latter, according to Article 109 paragraph 2, Article 85 paragraph 3 and Article 95 paragraph 1 of the Constitution respectively, is also a procedure for the triggering of executive responsibility. For its part, the motion of censure is not only a way to debate upon the Government's entire policy, but it may also result in the withdrawal of the mandate granted at investiture, while the assumption by the Government of its political responsibility represents not only a challenge for the triggering of a motion of censure but also a legislating procedure for, as has been shown, failure to initiate such a motion or rejection thereof has the effect that the presented draft of law shall be considered as passed, or, as the case may be, that the statement or programme shall be considered as accepted.

95. Finally, a third important function performed by Parliament is the *formation of certain State bodies*. There are various procedures for the formation of certain State bodies; generally, they are specially created for the body to which they refer. They are the result of the fact that investiture with certain functions shall be made by Parliament, exclusively or on proposal by another authority.

It is the Government that the main investiture procedure is related to. The candidate for the office of Prime Minister designated by the President of Romania shall, according to Article 103 paragraph 2 of the Constitution, within ten days after his designation, seek Parliament's vote of confidence upon the programme and complete list of the Government. For the purpose of the debate, the special Standing Commissions shall hear the candidates proposed to form the Government, checking whether there are major objections which would affect the granting of the vote of confidence. The candidate for the function of Prime Minister may, as a result of these hearings, substitute a person on the list, in conformity with the general principle that, as long as a proposal is not on the agenda, the initiator is entitled to withdraw or modify it. The vote of confidence must be given by the absolute majority of Parliament Members, after which the President of Romania is obliged to appoint the Government.

The Constitution provides that each Chamber shall appoint three of the nine judges of the Constitutional Court (Article 142 paragraph 2). In order to be elected for this office, the candidates are heard by each Chamber's Juridical Commission for Appointments and Immunities, which shall present, for each candidate, a brief characterization.

Article 133 of the Constitution provides that the Superior Council of Magistracy shall consist of nineteen members. Of these, fourteen are elected in the general meetings of the magistrates, and validated by the Senate; they belong to two sections, one for judges and one for public prosecutors (the former section consists of nine judges and the latter of five public prosecutors). The other two members of the Superior Council of Magistracy are representatives of civil society, specialists in law, who enjoy a good professional and moral reputation, elected by the Senate. They shall only participate in plenary proceedings. The remaining three members of the Superior Council of Magistracy are not elected. They are de jure members: the Minister of Justice, the president of the High Court of Cassation and Justice, and the General Public Prosecutor of the Public Prosecutor's Office attached to the High Court of Cassation and Justice.

Article 140 paragraph 4 of the Constitution provides that audit advisers shall be appointed by the Parliament for a term of office of nine years, which cannot be extended or renewed.

According to the Constitution of 1991, the two Chambers had the competence to make appointments and that competence was exercised separately or in joint session. The exception to the rule was the appointment of the People's Advocate Institution which, according to Article 55 paragraph 1 of the Constitution of 1991, was the exclusive competence of the Senate. The Constitution of 2003 modified this provision. Thus, according to its Article 58 corroborated by Article 65, the appointment of the People's Advocate Institution is the competence of both chambers.

It is not only the Constitution that regulates Parliament's competence to appoint certain public authorities. This competence is also regulated by various laws, such as the laws on election of some members of the National Council of the Audio-Visual Media, of the Managing Board of the State Property Fund, etc.

The usual procedure when Parliament's Chambers make appointments has two stages: the first consists of hearing the candidates before the commissions and the second of the debates in plenary session. As regards the proposals for the candidates, they are either made by a public authority, usually the President of Romania, or by the parliamentary groups where the law does not provide for the competence of such an authority.

96. The obvious conclusion to the entire previous discussion about the legislative power in Romania is that Parliament's precedence is the main characteristic feature of the constitutional political regime. It is based on the principle exposed in

Article 2 paragraph 1 of the Constitution, according to which national sovereignty resides with the Romanian people, who shall exercise it through their representative bodies and by referendum. Within the system of these bodies, as Article 61 paragraph 1 of the Constitution provides, Parliament is the supreme representative body of the Romanian people and the sole legislative authority of the State.

97. However, this presentation of Parliament's functions would not be complete without a few words about an important aspect related to the exercise of these functions, that is, the legislative delegation. According to Article 115 of the Constitution, Parliament may pass a special law enabling the Government to issue ordinances in fields outside the scope of organic laws, while under exceptional circumstances, the Government may issue an emergency ordinance. In the first case, the empowering law can impose upon the Government the obligation to submit the issued ordinances to Parliament for endorsement before the date when the empowering term is over, until expiration of the enabling term. In case the law does not provide for such an obligation, the ordinance need not be submitted for endorsement. This is mainly the case with general laws which, however, provide for the Government's obligation to detail its principles. In the second case, the ordinance becomes effective only after its submission to Parliament for endorsement, and, if the latter is not in session, it shall compulsorily be convened.

Ordinances can only be endorsed or rejected by means of a law.

It should be pointed out that legislative delegation is not a means to refrain Parliament, within the granted empowerment, from the exercise of its legislative function. It could hardly be so if one takes into account its constitutional status of unique legislative authority. It is only a means for the achievement of Parliament's legislative function in a special way, in two stages; the first one is governmental, while the second one, and also the decisive one, is parliamentary. For Parliament's Chambers, an ordinance submitted for endorsement is like a draft of law; they may pass it, with or without modifications, or reject it. The advantage lies in that it has had a previous period of application that could bring into relief the shortcomings of the regulation thus instituted.

Chapter 4. The Government

98. The Government is a public authority characterized by a collegiate, conjoined and hierarchic structure. Its constitutional status is characteristic of a parliamentary regime. In order to approach these aspects, we shall first deal with the formation of the Government.

One of the President's prerogatives is to designate a candidate to the office of Prime Minister, as a result of his consultation with the party which has obtained an absolute majority in Parliament, or – if no such majority exists – with the parties represented in Parliament (Article 85 paragraph 1 and Article 103 paragraph 1 of the Constitution). Designation is the expression of a special competence of the President of Romania, which he may exercise since the Government has a parliamentary origin, for it is formed on the basis of the vote of confidence given by Parliament. For this reason, the obligation to consult the party which has obtained an absolute majority in Parliament or, as the case may be, the parties represented in Parliament falls within the logic of the constitutional political regime. The designated candidate shall, within ten days, apply for Parliament's vote of confidence. After expiration of this term, the President may designate another candidate. The candidate may be a Parliament Member, for, according to Article 71 paragraph 2 of the Constitution, the office of Parliament Member is compatible with Government membership, or another personality who enjoys the confidence of the parliamentary majority.

99. According to the procedure, the candidate Ministers first have to be heard by the special parliamentary commissions. Then follows the vote of confidence. This procedure is meant not only to contribute to a better acquaintance of Parliament Members with the future Ministers but also to give the candidate for the office of Prime Minister the opportunity to substitute some of them, in order to avoid failures as much as possible. The debates and the vote of confidence concern the government programme and the list of Government members presented by the candidate to the office of Prime Minister. Government's investiture shall be made by the Chambers in joint session, based on the vote of the absolute majority of Deputies and Senators.

Once the vote of confidence has been obtained, the President of Romania appoints the Government. He has no freedom to refuse. After appointment, the Government members shall take the oath of faith before the President, and, as of that date, the exercise of their office becomes effective. In case of failure to form the Government within sixty days since the first application for investiture, as a result of failure to obtain the vote of confidence in at least two attempts, entitles the President of Romania to dissolve Parliament after consultations with the Presidents of the two Chambers and the leaders of the parliamentary groups.

Therefore, the Government's legitimacy is based on the mandate given by Parliament through a vote of confidence regarding the government programme and the list of Government members presented by the candidate to the office of Prime Minister.

100. The mandate ceases on the date general parliamentary elections are validated. This principle, contained in Article 110 paragraph 1 of the Constitution, is based on the fact that the Government's term of office is the very result of the logic of the investiture procedure: when Parliament, whose confidence was the basis for the formation and functioning of the Government, ceases its mandate, so does the Government. Cessation of the Government's mandate may also occur as a result of its dismissal. The Government may be dismissed in two cases: either following a withdrawal of confidence by Parliament, or as a result of the cessation of the office of Prime Minister or the latter's inability to exercise his powers for more than forty-five days.

Parliament can withdraw its confidence by passing a motion of censure, which has the effect that the majority by whose votes the Government was formed is lost; hence the necessity to form a new majority to invest in a new Government.

As regards cessation of the office of Prime Minister, according to Article 106 of the Constitution, this shall occur upon resignation, dismissal, disenfranchisement, incompatibility, death, or in all other cases provided for by law.

The Constitution provides in its Article 110 paragraph 4 that, in order to ensure continuity of the governmental activity, the Government whose mandate has ceased is bound to perform the necessary activity until the members of the new Government have taken the oath.

101. In case some members of the Government are dismissed by the President of Romania on proposal by the Prime Minister, the Government is reshuffled. A Government reshuffle may not include a change in the structure of the Government as endorsed by the Parliament on investiture, that is, the number of seats and their responsibilities. In case of a Government reshuffle, as well as vacancy of office, the President of Romania, also on proposal by the Prime Minister, shall appoint the new office holders. The Government's structure may also be modified as a result of a vacancy in the office of the Prime Minister. Cessation of the office held by a member of the Government may occur under the same circumstances as those presented for the cessation of the office of Prime Minister. The only difference is that, in addition, a Minister may be dismissed. In the event of vacancy of office, the President of Romania, on proposal by the Prime Minister, may appoint another member or, for a maximum period of forty-five days, may designate a member of the Government to substitute the one who cannot hold his office any longer. The same procedure shall apply in case a Minister is no longer in a position to exercise his powers.

As has already been mentioned, if the office of the Prime Minister becomes vacant, the entire Government shall be considered dismissed, and the interim Prime Minister shall lead the dismissed Government until the new Government has taken the oath. In case the interim Prime Minister was designated as a result of the fact that the office holder was not in a position to fulfil his tasks, after forty-five days, the Government shall also be considered dismissed, while it is bound to provide administration of public affairs until the new Government becomes effective. In the case of Ministers, after forty-five days, it is compulsory to have a new office holder appointed.

102. According to the definition given at the beginning of our discussion about the Government, the latter is a collegiate authority, different from its members. This is the result of the fact that the vote of confidence by which the Government has been invested refers to the whole list presented by the candidate to the office of Prime Minister. Therefore, it is the Government as a whole that is invested, not each particular member. Also related to its collegiate character is the conjoint political responsibility of the Government members for the Government's activity and for its actions. Since it is invested on the basis of Parliament's vote of confidence, the Government is politically responsible, according to Article 109 paragraph 1 of the Constitution, only before Parliament. Investiture and dismissal, as well as the political responsibility of the Government, are characteristic of the parliamentary regime. This is the reason why members of the Government may also be Parliament Members.

It was also pointed out that at the beginning of the chapter devoted to the Government that its structure is hierarchic. This hierarchy is based upon the Prime Minister's precedence in the management of the whole activity and the coordination of the members' activity. The Prime Minister's status results from the fact that it is he who has obtained the vote of confidence, as well as from certain special prerogatives: submission to Parliament of reports and statements for debate, proposal for the dismissal of certain members and appointment of others in case of a Government reshuffle or vacancy of office, the right to veto when the Government adopts an act, etc. This is the reason why cessation of the office of Prime Minister or the impossibility to exercise it for more than forty-five days incurs the Government's dismissal. There is a hierarchy among the other members of the Government, between State Ministers, who coordinate certain fields, and the other Ministers, who manage the structures of the ministries. These two capacities may be cumulated. Also, another hierarchic structure, this time narrower, is the Government's Executive Bureau, which is meant to solve problems in due time.

103. According to Article 105 paragraph 1 of the Constitution, membership of the Government shall be incompatible with the exercise of any other public office in authority, except the office of a Deputy or Senator. Likewise, it shall be incompatible with the exercise of any office of professional representation paid by a trading organization. This rule prohibits a Government member from holding another public office, with the exceptions mentioned for the Prime Minister and the interim Minister. According to the same Article, other incompatibilities shall be established by an organic law. This was done for such offices as those of judge, members of independent authorities of the public administration, such as the National Council of the Audio-Visual Media, etc.

Government members have a conjoint responsibility before Parliament; at the same time, they are criminally liable for acts committed in the exercise of their office. According to Article 109 paragraph 2 of the Constitution, only the Chamber of Deputies, the Senate and the President of Romania have the right to demand criminal prosecution against members of the Government for such acts. If such criminal prosecution has been requested, the President of Romania may decree that the Government member concerned be suspended from office. The case falls within the competence of the High Court of Cassation and Justice – as with Parliament Members or the President of Romania, for high treason.

104. The Government shall ensure the implementation of the domestic and foreign policy of the country and exercise the general management of public administration in accordance with its government programme accepted by Parliament (Article 102 paragraph 1[78] of the Constitution).[79]

One of the Government's constitutional obligations is that, in the exercise of its powers, it should cooperate with the social bodies concerned. To fulfil it, the Government created some special structures, such as the Government–Trade Unions Commission, which is actually a tripartite commission since it also includes representatives of the employers, and the Council for National Minorities, made up of representatives of the latter. At the same time, the Government has its own structure of services, including the Prime Minister's Cabinet, the Council for Reform and Economic Strategy, the Government's Secretariat General, the Department for the Relationship with Parliament led by a Minister responsible for the relations with Parliament, the Department for the Local Public Administration as part of the Government's Secretariat General, etc.

105. In the exercise of its powers, the Government adopts decisions and ordinances. Decisions shall be issued to organize the execution of laws. They have an individual or a normative character. Ordinances shall be issued under a special enabling law, within the limits and in conformity with the provisions thereof. Ordinances are the expression of a legislative competence delegated by Parliament, under Article 115 of the Constitution. According to this Article, the enabling law shall compulsorily establish the field and the date up to which ordinances can be issued. If the enabling law so requests, ordinances shall be submitted to Parliament for approval, according to the legislative procedure, until expiration of the enabling term.

According to Article 115 paragraph 4, in exceptional cases, the Government may adopt emergency ordinances. These shall come into force only after their submission to Parliament for approval. These ordinances shall be approved or rejected by a law which must also list the ordinances that ceased to be effective as a result of the expiration of the enabling term.

The decisions and the ordinances issued by the Government shall be signed by the Prime Minister and countersigned by the Ministers who are bound to execute them. They shall be published until expiration of the enabling term.

106. In the exercise of its powers, the Government has to establish relationships with the other actors involved in the political, social, economic and cultural life.

---

78. *See* the Decision No. 88/3.3.2004 of the Constitutional Court of Romania, published in Monitorul Oficial, Part I, No. 226/15.3.2004.
79. We would like to mention that in 2019 the Administrative Code was adopted, that regulated the general framework for the organization and functioning of the public administration authorities and entities. The related legislation refers to the Administrative Code, adopted by GEO No. 47/2019, published in the Monitorul Oficial, Part I, No. 555/5.7.2019, supplemented and modified (*see* Verginia Vedinaş, Codul Administrativ comentat. Explicaţii, jurisprudenţă, doctrina, Editura Universul Juridic, Bucureşti 2023, pp. 17 and the following, *see also* Ovidiu Podaru, *Codul administrativ*, ediţie îngrijită şi adnotată (Editura Hamangiu, Bucureşti, 2022, p. 9).

Among these, the most important one is the Government's relationship with Parliament. Given the Government's parliamentary origin, the *Government-Parliament relationship* is characteristic of these authorities in a parliamentary regime. For instance, the Government enjoys the right of legislative initiative, to which end it comes up with drafts of laws. On the basis of its right of legislative initiative, the Government also enjoys the right to come up with amendments. At request of the Government, Parliament may decide that the drafts of laws be passed under the rush procedure. However, as was seen before, the Government is subject to parliamentary control, mainly by means of questions, interpellations and parliamentary inquiries.

107. Since the Government is invested by Parliament, it shall function as long as it enjoys the support of the parliamentary majority that gave it the investiture votes. As a consequence, withdrawal of such support through a motion of censure, as an expression of the Government's political responsibility before Parliament, incurs its dismissal.

Motions of censure may occur either on Parliament's initiative or as a result of a risk assumed by the Government itself. When the motion of censure is initiated by Parliament Members, that is, at least one-third of their total number, it shall be debated upon, as with the investiture vote, by the Chambers in joint session. The motion may be passed by the absolute majority of the Deputies' and Senators' votes. When the motion of censure is provoked by the Government in case the latter assumes responsibility for a programme, a general policy statement, or a draft of law, the latter shall be considered passed unless a motion of censure is registered within three days since presentation or if such a motion is rejected. Thus, assumption by the Government of its responsibility is also a way to legislate under emergency circumstances, when the adoption of a law is essential for the fulfilment of the governmental programme. As part of this procedure, although the debate moves from the presented draft of law to the governmental policy, the draft may be improved on the basis of the amendments presented and accepted by the Government.

108. The Government-Parliament relationship is also characterized by the obligation of the former and of the other authorities of public administration to supply the information and the documents requested by the Chambers of Parliament or the parliamentary commissions, through the Presidents thereof. In case a legislative initiative implies modifications of the State budget or the State social security budget, the request for information shall be compulsory.

If they wish, members of the Government are entitled to attend Parliament's sessions. This also implies the right to speak, meaning that Ministers may intervene in order to expose their viewpoint, whatever the stage of the debating procedure – in Plenum or in commissions. However, in case they are so requested, they are bound to attend.

A flexible separation of powers between the legislative and the executive is characteristic of the Government-Parliament relationship in a parliamentary regime. In this respect, the Government, with a view to fulfil its programme, participates in the legislative work of Parliament, mainly by exercising its right to legislative initiative and by participation in the debates, while it is politically responsible before Parliament. Conversely, the Chambers of Parliament play the role of censors of the governmental activity, in order that the latter be fulfilled in conformity with the will of the parliamentary majority on the basis of which the Government was invested.

109. Another important relationship that the Government establishes is its relationship with the local authorities. It transfers some competencies based on the principle of subsidiarity through şlaws and methodologies. Since the local authorities – the Mayors and the Local Councils – are elected through universal suffrage by the citizens in their respective localities, they are autonomous, being a local structure that represents a counterbalance to the State's central administration.

Nevertheless, Article 102 paragraph 1 of the Constitution stipulates that it is the Government that exercises the general management of public administration. On the basis of this general competence, governmental decisions are also compulsory for the local bodies. According to Article 123 of the Constitution, the Government appoints a Prefect in each county and in the municipality of Bucharest, who is its local representative. In this capacity, the Prefect may challenge, before the administrative court, the acts of the local bodies which he deems illegal. The challenged act is suspended de jure.

The Government may dismiss the Local Council, or the Mayor or a local Councillor, only for extremely serious acts, on proposal by the Prefect. The dismissal decision may be challenged by the interested parties before the administrative court. As a result of the dismissal of the Local Council, the Mayor or a local Councillor, new elections shall be organized.

Relevant aspects regarding the organisation, functioning and the competencies of public administration authorities and institutions, the statute of personnel, administrative liability, public services and specific rules regarding the private and public property of the state and of the territorial administrative units can be found within the Administrative Code, adopted on 3 July 2019, most recently amended by Government Emergency Ordinance (GEO) 31/21.3.2024.

110. While exercising its powers, the Government establishes relationships not only with the local authorities but also with the central public administration. Ministries are subordinated to the Government. The latter, like the ministries, may have certain subordinated administrative structures, such as agencies, State secretariats, etc. Such structures may also function independently, in which case they can only be established under law.

The principles governing the authorities of the central public administration are hierarchic subordination and decentralization. According to the first principle, there is a strict hierarchy, from the Prime Minister down to the basis of the administrative structure of the State apparatus. According to the second principle, certain competencies are delegated by the central bodies to the decentralized public services within the territory, as well as, at the governmental level, to the Prefects. The Prefects, according to Article 123 paragraph 2 of the Constitution, head the decentralized public services of the ministries and of the other central bodies in the administrative-territorial units in which they perform their activity.

Chapter 5. The Judicial Authority

111. Chapter VI of the Constitution of 2003 is devoted to the judicial authority. After almost half a century of totalitarian regimes, the Constitution proclaims the basic principles for the achievement of justice in Article 124, which provides that 'justice shall be rendered in the name of the law' and 'judges shall be independent and subject only to the law'.

According to the Constitution, justice is achieved by the High Court of Cassation and Justice and the other courts of law, as established by the law. At present, that is Law No. 303/2004 on the status of judges and prosecutors (as amended).

112. According to these laws, the judicial power shall be separate from the other powers of the State, having its own prerogatives exercised through courts of law and the Public Ministry, in accordance with the principles and dispositions provided in the Constitution. It is also provided that the courts of law shall carry out justice for the purpose of defending and achieving the fundamental rights and freedoms of the citizens, as well as other legitimate rights and interests referred to them. The courts shall try all the cases regarding civil, commercial, labour, family, administrative, and penal juridical relations, as well as any other cases for which the law has not established another competent body.

The Public Ministry emerged as a result of the reorganization of the old Prosecutor's Office. In this respect, the Constitution provides in its Article 131 that, within the judiciary, it shall represent the general interests of society and defend the legal order, as well as the citizens' rights and freedoms. The Public Ministry shall discharge its powers through Public Prosecutors, constituted into public prosecutor's offices in accordance with the law.

113. The Judicial Organization Act has a number of general provisions, including several general principles for the administration of justice. Thus, it is provided that judges shall be independent and subject only to the law. No one is above the law. Justice shall be equal for everyone, without discrimination on the basis of race, nationality, ethnic origin, language, religion, sex, opinion, political affiliation, fortune, or social origin. Court sittings shall be public, except in the cases provided by law.

Another important provision is that the judicial procedure shall be held in Romanian. Citizens belonging to national minorities, as well as persons who cannot understand or speak Romanian, have the right to take cognizance of all acts and files of the case, to speak before the court, and to formulate conclusions through an interpreter; in criminal trials, this right shall be ensured free of charge. In all actions at law, the parties shall have the right to be represented or assisted, as the case may be, by legal counsel.

114. As far as the structure and operation of the courts of law are concerned, according to the system introduced by Law Nos 303/2004[80] and 304/2004,[81] the courts of law are: courts of first instance; tribunals; courts of appeal; and the High Court of Cassation and Justice. A particular case is that of martial law courts, which shall also function within the limits established by law.

The first category is that of courts of first instance. The courts of first instance shall function in every county and in the municipality of Bucharest. As a rule, the cases falling under the competence of first-instance judges shall be ruled by panels of two judges. Exceptions to the rule are certain cases of lesser interest, which shall be ruled by a single judge.

115. The second category in the list given above is that of tribunals. A tribunal shall function in each county and in the municipality of Bucharest; the constituency of each tribunal shall include all courts of first instance in the respective county or in the municipality of Bucharest. With the exception of the cases which, according to the law, shall be ruled in the first resort by the tribunals, the latter function as courts of appeal. It is worth mentioning that under the new law, as well as in parallel modifications of the civil and criminal procedure codes, an appeal may be attacked. This attack had been known to the Romanian inter-war legislation but had been eliminated by the totalitarian regime. In their capacity as courts of appeal, tribunals rule on recourses against the decisions pronounced by the courts of first instance. According to the law, their decisions are not subject to appeal.

It was shown above that cases at first instance are ruled by panels of two judges. Appeals and recourses are ruled by panels of three judges.

According to the legal provisions, fifteen courts of appeal have been established; the constituency of each Court of Appeal includes two– three counties. They rule, as courts of appeal, on the appeals declared against the decisions pronounced at first instance by the tribunals. They also rule, as recourse instances, on the applications for recourse filed against the decisions pronounced in appeal by the tribunals.

116. The High Court of Cassation and Justice is the highest body of the Romanian judicial system. Organization and functioning of the High Court of Cassation and Justice are dealt with by Law Nos 303/2022[82] and 304/2022.[83]

The law provides that the High Court of Cassation and Justice pursues the correct and unitary application of the laws by all courts.

Subject to recourse before the High Court of Cassation and Justice are the decisions by the courts of appeal, as well as other decisions established by the law. It also rules on recourses in the interest of the law and repeals remedies ruled against judicial decisions and acts. It also has a special competence of ruling on the merits

80. This law has been expressly abolished by Law No. 303/15.11.2022, published in the Monitorul Oficial, Part I, No. 1102/16.11.2022.
81. This law has been expressly abolished by Law No. 304/15.11.2022, published in the Monitorul Oficial, Part I, No. 1104/16.11.2022.
82. Published in the Monitorul Oficial, Part I, No. 1102/16.11.2022.
83. Published in the Monitorul Oficial, Part I, No. 1104/16.11.2022.

in certain cases provided for by the law. A peculiarity with respect to the competence of the High Court of Cassation and Justice is its right to intimate the Constitutional Court for deciding on the constitutionality of laws prior to promulgation (preventive control). Another prerogative is that at the end of each year, in joint sections, the Court establishes which cases demanding improvement of the legislation are and notifies the Ministry of Justice in this respect.

In the exercise of their powers, judges shall be independent and subject only to the law. The President, the Vice President, the section Presidents and the Judges are State Officials and may not be dismissed during their term of office. The Court's activity is mainly performed in sections, each with its own competencies. These sections are: Civil, Criminal, Commercial, Administrative Proceedings, and Military.

Alongside the High Court of Cassation and Justice, the Public Prosecutor's Office attached to the High Court of Cassation and Justice operates, headed by the General Prosecutor. The latter attends the joint section meetings of the Court, as well as any panel of the Court when he deems it necessary.

§1. The Public Ministry

117. According to Article 131 of the Constitution of 2003 (former Article 130 in the Constitution of 1991), within the judicial activity, the Public Ministry represents the general interests of society and defends the legal order, as well as the citizens' rights and freedoms, as it exerts its functions according to the law.[84] It discharges its powers through public prosecutors, constituted into public prosecutor's offices, in accordance with the law. The public prosecutor's offices are attached to courts of law; they direct and supervise the criminal investigation activity of the police, according to the law.

The activity of public prosecutors is organized according to the principles of legality, impartiality and hierarchic control (Article 132 paragraph 1). At the same time, the office of public prosecutor is incompatible with any other public or private office, except for academic activities (Article 132 paragraph 2).

118. The Public Ministry's role is accomplished in several ways. First of all, it is responsible for the conduct of the criminal investigation and, as the case may be, the surveillance thereof. To this end, prosecutors conduct and control the criminal investigation activity carried on by the police and other bodies, all of which are obliged to comply with the dispositions of the prosecutor as provided for by the law.

The Public Ministry institutes trials before courts of law in criminal cases, brings civil actions in the cases provided for by the law, and participates, if allowed by the law, in the trial of cases by courts of law. Of course, the Public Ministry is also entitled, as provided by the law, to appeal against judicial decisions. It is also the task of the Public Ministry to supervise the observance of the law in the enforcement of judicial decisions and other writs of execution, in places of preventive detention, in execution of the punishments, and in respect of educational and safety measures.

84. *See* Ch. II in Law No. 304/2022.

The defence of the rights and interests of juveniles and of persons laid under a judicial interdiction is a special prerogative of the Public Ministry as well.

And last but not least, the Public Ministry also has the task to study the causes that generate or favour criminality and to present proposals for the elimination thereof.

A characteristic feature of Prosecutor's Offices is that they are independent of the courts of law. According to the principle of hierarchy and hierarchical control, the prosecutors of each Prosecutor's Office are subordinated to the Head of that Prosecutor's Office, while the latter is subordinated to the head of the hierarchically higher Prosecutor's Office in the same territorial area. The hierarchically superior prosecutor may perform any of the prerogatives of the prosecutors subordinated to him and may suspend or annul their acts or decisions if they conflict with the law.

Even though the dispositions of the hierarchically superior public prosecutor, given in accordance with the law, are compulsory for the subordinate public prosecutors, the latter are free to present before the court the conclusions he deems founded. Likewise, the dispositions of the Minister of Justice, given through the agency of the Public Prosecutor General with a view to the observance and application of the law, are compulsory as well. The Minister of Justice exercises control over all members of the Public Ministry, through the inspector-public prosecutors from the Public Prosecutor General's Office attached to the High Court of Cassation and Justice and from the public prosecutor's offices attached to the courts of appeal, or other delegated public prosecutors.

119. Public prosecutor's offices are attached to courts of first instance, tribunals and courts of appeal. They are headed by the Public Prosecutor General's Office, attached to the High Court of Cassation and Justice and led by the Public Prosecutor General, assisted by two deputies. Therefore, the Public Prosecutor General exercises control over all prosecutor's offices. He participates in the meetings of the High Court of Cassation and Justice in joint sections and designates from among the members of the Public Prosecutor General's Office attached to the High Court of Cassation and Justice those prosecutors who shall participate in the meetings of the Constitutional Court.

§2. The Bar

120. The organization and the activity of lawyers are regulated under Law No. 51/1995,[85] amended several times, most recently by Law No. 32/11.1.2023[86] and by Law No. 89/2023[87]

According to Article 50, the bar is made up of all the lawyers in the county of the municipality of Bucharest. The headquarters of the bar is in the county seat of the respective county; for the municipality of Bucharest, it is in Bucharest.

85. Republished in the Monitorul Oficial, Part I, No. 440/24.5.2018.
86. Published in the Monitorul Oficial, Part I, No. 36/12.1.2023.
87. Published in the Monitorul Oficial, Part I, No. 310/12.4.2023.

Article 49 of the law provides that a lawyer's profession is organized and functions according to the principle of autonomy, within the limits of the competencies provided by the law. Election of the steering bodies of lawyers' bars is only made by secret ballot. The steering bodies of a bar are: (a) the General Assembly; (b) the Council; (c) the Dean (Article 51).

121. The General Assembly has the following competencies: takes measures for the exercise of the lawyer's profession by the respective Bar Association; elects and dismisses the Dean, the Council members, the members of the Audit Commission, and the Discipline Commission; elects the Bar Association's delegates to the Lawyers' Congress; approves the draft budget and clears the Council in relation to its activity and to the funds it administrated.

122. The Council consists of five to fifteen members, elected for a four-year period, from among the lawyers who have a minimum uninterrupted practice of eight years (Article 56 paragraph 1 of Law No. 51/1995 with its subsequent amendments and supplementations). The Dean and the Deputy Dean are counted as members. The Bar Association's Council has several powers, including (the list is not exhaustive):

1. adopts measures for the application and observance of Law No. 51/1995;
2. fulfils the decisions made by the Council of the Romanian National Union of Bar Associations and by the General Assembly;
3. elaborates, modifies and publishes the annual table of lawyers, members of the Bar Association, and communicates it to those entitled;
4. adopts measures for the organization of the professional, disciplinary and deontological control, for the resolution of petitions and complaints, as provided by the law and the Statute of the Association;
5. checks and takes note if the legal conditions are met in relation to applications for acceptance to the professional association and approves such acceptance either on the basis of an exam or not;
6. makes decisions in relation to the status of incompatibility or the end of incompatibility;
7. makes decisions in relation to applications for transfer to another job;
8. organizes and guides the activity of the legal assistance services in the county, as provided by the law and the Statute of the Association;
9. intimates the Discipline Commission about lawyers' infractions of discipline;
10. suspends from exercise of office the lawyer who fails to pay the taxes and the money contributions provided by the law;
11. solves challenges against the Dean's decision regarding the fee for professional services;
12. establishes the lawyer's quota for the Bar's budget;
13. approves the personnel records and the payroll;
14. elaborates the draft annual budget, submits it to the General Assembly and administers the Bar's patrimony;
15. submits to the General Assembly the annual report, the current fund administration report and the Bar's patrimony administration report;

16. elects the Bar's Deputy Dean; and
17. solves the complaints and the challenges against the Dean's decisions.

123. The Dean is elected for a four-year mandate and can be re-elected only once. He has to be elected from among the lawyers having a minimum experience of ten years.

The Dean has the following powers/competencies:

1. represents the Bar in its relationships with domestic or foreign natural and legal persons;
2. convenes and presides over the Council's meetings;
3. approves the applications for free of charge legal assistance;
4. exercises the remedies at law against the decisions made by the Discipline Commission and by the Council in those cases for which such remedies are provided by the law;
5. acts as chief accountant for the Bar's expenditures;
6. takes measures related to the management of the Bar which are beyond the competence of the General Assembly or that of the Council; and
7. fulfils any other tasks provided by the law or by the steering bodies of the Romanian National Union of Bar Associations and put under his competence.

The Deputy Dean replaces the Dean on request by or in the absence of the latter.

The Union and the bars perform an independent activity and are in no way subordinated to the Ministry of Justice.

124. During the trial, the lawyer holds a position that is equal to that of the prosecutor, since the right to defence is enshrined by the Constitution in its Article 24, which provides that the right to defence is guaranteed and that throughout the trial the parties shall have the right to be assisted by a lawyer of their own choice or appointed ex officio.

Similar provisions to those laid down under Article 24 can be found in the Charter of Fundamental Rights of the European Union (CFREU; Article 48 – Presumption of innocence and right of defence).

§3. The Status of Magistrates

125. According to the law, the body of magistrates is made up of the judges from all the courts of law, the public prosecutors attached to these courts within the framework of the public prosecutor's offices, as well as the assistant magistrates of the High Court of Cassation and Justice, all of whom have the quality of magistrates.

Article 125 of the Constitution stipulates that judges are appointed by the President of Romania and that they shall be irremovable, according to the law. The appointment proposals, as well as the promotion, transfer of, and sanctions against judges, shall only be within the competence of the Superior Council of Magistracy, under the terms of its organic law.

It is also provided that the office of a judge shall be incompatible with any other public or private office, except that of an academic professional activity, a provision that is reiterated by Article 132(2) in relation to prosecutors.

According to the Law on Judicial Organization, the hierarchy in the framework of the body of magistrates of executive functions shall be established in relation to the level of their qualification and their length of service, by the professional grades provided by the law. However, the hierarchy of the leading functions within the framework of the body of magistrates shall be established in relation to the level of the courts and of the public prosecutor's offices. The Minister of Justice, his deputies (State Secretaries) and the juridical specialized personnel from the Ministry of Justice shall be assimilated to magistrates throughout their term of office.

As was pointed out above, judges and prosecutors, with the exception of those on probation, are appointed by Decree by the President of Romania, on proposal by the Superior Council of Magistracy. Courts of first instances and the prosecutor's offices attached to them may employ judges and prosecutors on probation appointed under an Order by the Minister of Justice.

126. The prosecutors on probation are appointed on proposal by the Public Prosecutor General. Probation for judges and prosecutors shall be two years. A person with a law degree takes a competitive exam for the National Institute of Magistracy, attends it for one year and then becomes a trainee judge for one more year. They must remain judges or prosecutors for a ten-year period. After completing their probation term, magistrates on probation have to stand for the qualification examination. The results of this examination shall be communicated by the examination board of the Ministry of Justice, which shall notify the Superior Council of Magistracy in this respect. The latter, after validation of the examinations and centralization of the data, prepares the classification table of the candidates in the order of their marks and, on the basis thereof, makes appointments for the vacant offices, the candidates being able to choose their office on the basis of their results in the examination.

127. According to the law, a magistrate's promotion to a higher office depends on several conditions. He should have a worthwhile activity attested by qualifying marks given by his hierarchical superiors and the inspectors and shall meet certain length-of-service conditions which vary in terms of the importance of the office.

Promotion and transfer of judges shall be ordered by the Superior Council of Magistracy, and of prosecutors on proposal by the Public Prosecutor General.

§4. The Superior Council of Magistracy

128. The Constitution provides in its Articles 133–134 the structure and the powers of the Superior Council of Magistracy.

As was mentioned before, Article 133 of the Constitution provides that the Superior Council of Magistracy shall consist of nineteen members. Of these, fourteen are elected in the general assemblies of the magistrates, and validated by the Senate; they belong to two sections, one for judges and one for public prosecutors (the former section consists of nine judges, and the latter of five public prosecutors). The other two members of the Superior Council of Magistracy are representatives of the civil society, law experts, who enjoy a good professional and moral reputation, elected by the Senate. They shall only participate in plenary proceedings. The remaining three members of the Superior Council of Magistracy are not elected. They are de jure members: the Minister of Justice, the president of the High Court of Cassation and Justice, and the General Public Prosecutor of the Public Prosecutor's Office attached to the High Court of Cassation and Justice.

According to Article 133, paragraph 3, the President of the Superior Council of Magistracy is elected for a one-year mandate, which may not be renewed, from among the magistrates provided under Article 133, paragraph 2, letter (a), while paragraph 4 specifies that the members of the Superior Council of Magistracy shall have a six-year mandate.

This constitutional regulation is completely new and is the result of the revision of 2003. The need to change the text referring to the Superior Council of Magistracy came from the fact that the old text proved quite unsuccessful, which reflected negatively on the functioning of this body, which is a constitutive part of the judicial authority.

This is the reason why it was decided that the role of this body is to guarantee the independence of justice. This function as a guarantor can be achieved, on the one hand, by the way it is formed and organized and, on the other hand, by what this body actually does.

129. The composition of the Superior Council of Magistracy is so conceived as to reflect the very structure of the judicial authority and achieve the connection with the civil society. It is important that the judges and the prosecutors are elected in the general assemblies of the magistrates. By that, they are genuine representatives of those who democratically designate them. Besides the judges and the prosecutors, the Council also includes two representatives of civil society, specialists in law, enjoying a high professional and moral reputation. They are elected by the Senate of Romania and may only participate in the plenary sessions.

As was seen, the constitutional text stipulates that the Council includes the Minister of Justice, the President of the High Court of Cassation and Justice, and the Prosecutor General of the Public Prosecutor's Office attached to the High Court of Cassation and Justice. Their inclusion among the members of the Council is natural because, given their powers within the judicial authority, they have to be familiar with all the problems and the preoccupations in the field. Nevertheless, the Constitution also imposes certain limits with regard to their participation in the Council's activity.

The constitutional text also gave a solution to the election of the Council's President, an issue that had remained unsolved by the old text of 1991. Thus, the office shall be held by a magistrate elected from among the members of the Council. It is a one-year mandate which may not be renewed. It is also worth mentioning that the Council's sessions will be presided over by the President of Romania in case he participates.

As far as the acts by which the Superior Council of Magistracy exercises its powers are concerned, they are called decisions. Two rules govern these decisions: (1) they are made by secret ballot; and (2) they are final and irrevocable, with the exception of the disciplinary ones.

130. The Superior Council of Magistracy has two important functions: to propose to the President of Romania the appointment of judges and public prosecutors, and to perform the role of a court of law, by means of its sections, as regards the disciplinary liability of judges and public prosecutors in case they commit illegal acts that are disciplinary offences.

In relation to the first function, the constitutional text brings in certain clarifications. Thus, the Council shall not propose trainees to be appointed as judges or prosecutors. Article 134 paragraph 1 should be corroborated with Article 125, while the legal status of trainees being different. Moreover, since trainee judges are not appointed by the President of Romania, they do not enjoy the immovability provided under Article 125.

The article devoted to the second function (that of a disciplinary court of law) is more detailed. First, the Constitution gives the Council the power of a court of law in the field of disciplinary accountability. This role is achieved by means of the two sections, one for judges and the other for prosecutors. These sections function according to the provisions of Law No. 305/2022 on the Superior Council of Magistracy.[88]

In order to secure genuine independence and impartiality to the two sections, the Constitution wisely gives no right to vote to the Minister of Justice, to the President of the High Court of Cassation and Justice and to the Prosecutor General, even though they are de jure members of the Superior Council of Magistracy.

Article 134 should be corroborated with Article 21 of the Constitution on the free access to justice. Thus, paragraph 3 allows that the Council's disciplinary decisions could be challenged before the High Court of Cassation and Justice. Also wisely and prudently, Article 134 was added paragraph 4, which allows for the organic law to establish other powers as well. This way, the text allows for receptivity in relation to the new issues that may be faced in future by the achievement of the Council's role to guarantee the independence of justice.

§5. The Constitutional Court

131. Articles 142–147 of the Constitution are devoted to the Constitutional Court. Its purpose is to serve as the guarantor for the supremacy of the Constitution.

It is made up of nine judges, appointed for a nine-year mandate that cannot be renewed or extended. Three judges are appointed by the Chamber of Deputies, three by the Senate, and three by the President of Romania. One-third of the judges of the Court are renewed every three years, each authority entitled to do so by designating one judge. Accordingly, the first judges were appointed for three, six, and nine years

88. Published in the Monitorul Oficial, Part I, No. 1105/16.12.2022.

respectively, the Chamber of Deputies, the Senate and the President of Romania designating one judge for each of these periods.

The Chambers of Parliament elect the judges, after they have been heard, on proposal by the Standing Bureaus, on the basis of the recommendation by the Juridical Commission and the nominations proposed by the parliamentary groups.

Article 143 of the Constitution stipulates that the judges of the Constitutional Court must have graduated from law, and have high professional competence and at least eighteen years of experience in juridical or academic activities in law.

Law No. 47/1992 (as amended by Law No. 177/2010), which is the organic law for the organization and functioning of the Constitutional Court, provides that the judges begin to exercise their office on the date when the oath of allegiance is taken before the President of Romania and the Presidents of the two Chambers of Parliament.

According to the law, the mandate of these judges should be characterized by two main features: independence and immovability. Also, they may not be made responsible for the opinions and the votes expressed in their decisions.

132. Article 146 of the Constitution lays down the competencies of the Constitutional Court. These are to:

1. adjudicate on the constitutionality of laws, before the promulgation thereof upon notification by the President of Romania, one of the presidents of the two Chambers, the Government, the High Court of Cassation and Justice, the People's Advocate Institution, a number of at least fifty deputies or at least twenty-five senators, as well as ex officio, on initiatives to revise the Constitution;
2. adjudicate on the constitutionality of treaties or other international agreements, upon notification by one of the presidents of the two Chambers, a number of at least fifty deputies or at least twenty-five senators;
3. adjudicate on the constitutionality of the Standing Orders of Parliament, upon notification by the president of either Chamber, by a parliamentary group or a number of at least fifty Deputies or at least twenty-five Senators;
4. decide on objections as to the unconstitutionality of laws and ordinances, brought up before courts of law or commercial arbitration; the objection as to the unconstitutionality may also be brought up directly by the People's Advocate Institution;
5. solve legal disputes of a constitutional nature between public authorities, at the request of the President of Romania, one of the presidents of the two Chambers, the Prime Minister, or the president of the Superior Council of Magistracy;
6. guard the observance of the procedure for the election of the President of Romania and to confirm the ballot returns;
7. ascertain the circumstances which justify the interim in the exercise of the office of President of Romania, and to report its findings to Parliament and the Government;
8. give advisory opinion on the proposal to suspend from office the President of Romania;

9. guard the observance of the procedure for the organization and holding of a referendum, and to confirm its returns;
10. check the compliance with the conditions for the exercise of the legislative initiative by citizens;
11. decide on the objections of unconstitutionality of a political party; and
12. carry out other duties stipulated by the organic law of the Court.

Therefore, the Court acts as a constitutional judge, an electoral judge for presidential elections, and a constitutional authority. It has a strictly interpretative competence. According to the law, the Court's competence cannot be challenged by any authority, while the Court is the only one to decide about its competence, within the limits provided by the Constitution.

133. Acting as a constitutional judge, the Court has a jurisdictional competence exercising an *a priori* and *a posteriori* control of the law.[89]

The *a priori* control lies in the fact that the Court may be intimated with an objection of unconstitutionality of the adopted law, prior to its promulgation, formulated by the President of Romania, the President of either Chamber of Parliament, the High Court of Cassation and Justice through its united departments, by the Government, or by at least fifty Deputies or twenty-five Senators. While the objection of unconstitutionality is being solved, the term for the promulgation shall be interrupted.

Before making any decision on the objection, the Court is bound to request the Government's and the two Chambers' viewpoints. The Court shall decide on the objection by a vote of the majority of its judges. The quorum for the plenum to be legal is two-thirds of the number of judges. If the Court finds that the law or some of the provisions which were subject to control are unconstitutional, the decision pronounced shall be notified to the two Chambers of Parliament for reconsideration of the entire law or its unconstitutional provisions. In case, after reconsideration, each Chamber passes the law in its original form by a two-thirds majority, the objection of unconstitutionality is rejected and promulgation becomes compulsory. If such a majority is not met, the law shall be submitted for promulgation without the provisions declared to be unconstitutional, or, if unconstitutionality refers to the entire law, the latter shall not be submitted for promulgation again.

134. The *a posteriori* control lies in the control upon the constitutionality of the parliamentary statutes – the Chamber of Deputies' Statute, the Senate's Statute and the Statute for joint sessions – and through the decisions on objections of unconstitutionality brought before the courts of law.

When requested to make a pronouncement upon the constitutionality of the parliamentary statutes, the Court can be intimated by either Parliament's Chamber, by

89. 'The constitutional contentious court case law regarding the admissibility of preliminary intimation has evolved in time, and today the Constitutional Court may intimate such preliminary questions, no matter the kind of control in question, a priori or a posteriori.' (Marian Enache, in *Evoluţia dreptului Uniunii Europene: Dialogul între Curtea de Justiţie a Uniunii Europene şi Curţile Constituţionale*, 3 Oct. 2022, www.juridice.ro, accessed on 25 Feb. 2023).

a parliamentary group, or by at least fifty Deputies or twenty-five Senators. Prior to solving the intimation, the Court is bound to request the viewpoint of the Standing Bureau of the Chamber whose Statute is being controlled. The competence to decide on the intimation lies with the Court's plenum. The decision shall be pronounced by the vote of the majority of the judges and shall be notified to the Chamber whose Statute has been debated upon, which must then make it comply with the constitutional provisions.

Within the *a posteriori* control, one may notice that the Constitutional Court of Romania, considering that during the European constitutionalization process, an important role lies with the preliminary intimation submitted by the Constitutional Courts, formulated such a preliminary intimation, for the first time in 2017, in a case stipulated in the Constitutional Court Decision No. 534/18.7.2018.

135. Courts of law can make their own contribution to the exercise of the constitutionality control. This is illustrated by the fact that an objection of unconstitutionality may be raised by a court of law ex officio or on request by the parties. Intimation of the Court shall be made through a conclusion which shall also include the opinion of the court of law about the invoked objection of unconstitutionality.

The objection of unconstitutionality may be solved either on the merits or on appeal. To this end, the President of the Court establishes panels for the merits, formed of three judges, and panels for the appeal, formed of five judges, different from those who decide on the merits.

When the objection is solved on the merits, the President of the Panel, designated when the latter was established, shall designate a judge as rapporteur. The rapporteur-judge has the task to prepare the judgment session, and is bound to request the Government's and the two Chambers' viewpoints upon the objection, as well as any other necessary information and documentation. Also, for the same purpose, the rapporteur-judge shall make a report concerning the problems related to the constitutional objection, including the viewpoints, the received documentation and information, as well as the doctrine and the practice relevant to the case.

It is possible that the rapporteur-judge should find the objection to be obviously unfounded. In such a case, he may make a preliminary report on the basis of which the President of the Panel shall convene the judges to deliberate. In such a case, the request for the above-mentioned public authorities' viewpoints is not compulsory, and the judgment shall be given without the parties being heard. By unanimity of votes, the Panel can reject the objection as obviously unfounded. If the objection is not obviously unfounded, however, either because the rapporteur-judge has not deemed it so and has made his final report to that effect, or because no unanimity was reached, the President of the Panel establishes a date for the judgment and orders convening of the parties and of the Public Ministry. The judgment shall take place in public session, according to the rules of civil procedure that shall be applied accordingly. The parties can be represented by lawyers entitled to plead before the High Court of Cassation and Justice.

The parties and the Public Ministry can make recourse against the Court's decision within ten days since notification – both in case the objection was rejected as obviously unfounded and in case another decision was pronounced as a result of the debates during the judgment session. The recourse shall always be solved in a public session, with the parties and the Public Ministry being convened. In this case, designation of a rapporteur-judge is not compulsory, for the judgment takes place on the basis of the previously requested viewpoints. Nevertheless, if the objection had been rejected as obviously unfounded and without the viewpoints of the public authorities provided for by the law – the Government and the two Parliament's Chambers – being requested, are to be requested now. At the same time, the Panel can request any other information and material it deems necessary. Once the recourse is accepted, the Court shall rule on appeal on the objection of unconstitutionality.

136. In terms of constitutional jurisdiction, the Court also has competence to solve challenges regarding the constitutionality of a political party.[90] In this case, the Court can be intimated by the President of either Chamber of Parliament on the basis of a decision adopted by the vote of the majority of the Chamber's members, or by the Government. To solve the challenge, the President of the Court shall designate a judge as rapporteur, who is bound to notify the party whose constitutionality is challenged about it and provide the evidence on which the challenge is based to that party. The latter may submit, before the date specified by the rapporteur-judge, a defending report, accompanied by adequate evidence.

The unconstitutionality of a political party is based on the provisions of Article 40 paragraph 2 of the Constitution referring to the right of association, according to which any political parties or organizations which, by their aims or activity, militate against political pluralism, the principles of a State governed by the rule of law, or against the sovereignty, integrity or independence of Romania shall be unconstitutional. The challenge has to be judged by the Court's Plenum, with the parties and the Public Ministry being convened, on the basis of the report presented by the rapporteur-judge and of the administered evidence, while the decision shall be pronounced by the vote of the majority of judges. If the challenge is accepted, the Tribunal of the Municipality of Bucharest shall be notified to delete the respective political party from the register of legally established parties.

All final decisions by the Constitutional Court, pronounced by the latter in its capacity as a body of constitutional jurisdiction, shall be published in the *Monitorul Oficial of Romania* and are – according to Article 147 of the Constitution – binding for the future.

137. As was mentioned before, in its capacity as an electoral judge, the Constitutional Court has competence to solve challenges formulated during presidential elections, establish the result of the voting, and, when required, establish the date for the second ballot. It also validates the result of the elections for the office of President of Romania. The decisions pronounced shall be published in the *Monitorul Oficial of Romania.*

90. *See* Ioan Vida, *Curtea Constituţională, justiţia politicului sau politica justiţiei?* (Editura Monitorul Oficial, Bucureşti, 2010), pp. 17 and the following.

138. Finally, the Court also acts as a constitutional authority. In this capacity, it shall make ex officio pronouncements about initiatives for the revision of the Constitution. To this end, the draft of law or the legislative proposal, as the case may be, shall be submitted to the Constitutional Court which is bound, by the vote of two-thirds of its judges, to make a pronouncement in plenary session about the proposal for revision through a decision that shall be notified to the initiators and published in the *Monitorul Oficial of Romania.* The proposal for revision shall be submitted to Parliament only accompanied by the Court's decision.

139. As part of its capacity as constitutional authority, the Court shall also ascertain the circumstances that justify the interim in the exercise of the office of President of Romania, and shall notify Parliament and the Government. Vacancy of office shall be acknowledged on request by the President of either Chamber of Parliament or by the interim President exercising the powers of the President of Romania during the period the latter is suspended from office. If the interim is owed to the President's temporary incapacity to exercise his powers, the request may also be formulated by the latter. The decision by the Court shall be adopted by the Plenum, by the vote of the majority of judges.

140. It is possible that the Chairman of the joint session of Parliament's Chambers should request the Constitutional Court to pronounce its approval on the proposal that the President of Romania be suspended from office. In such a case, the approval shall be given by the Court's Plenum, by the vote of the majority of judges, on the basis of a report prepared by three judges, designated by the President of the Court upon receiving the intimation and on the basis of his investigations in preparing the session. The President of Romania shall be notified about the date established for the debates and can give explanations about the acts he is held responsible for. The approval, which has a consultative character, shall be notified to the Presidents of both Chambers of Parliament and to the President of Romania.

It should also be mentioned that the Constitutional Court has competence to check whether the procedure for the organization and development of a referendum is observed and to confirm the results thereof. Likewise, it has competence to check whether the requirements for the exercise by the citizens of their right to legislative initiative are met, in conformity with Article 74 paragraph 1 and Article 150 of the Constitution.

Chapter 6. Independent Non-political Institutions

141. The protection of human rights, equality of rights of all citizens without any distinction as to ethnic origin, privatization and the safeguarding of rights and freedoms of the unions are constitutional provisions that led to the establishment, either under the law or under decisions by the Government, of several advisory bodies, whose task is to assist either the legislative or the executive in the fulfilment of their duties. They have the power to issue advisory opinions, which are not binding for the bodies that request them. Even so, practice has proved that they have a strong impact on the social and economic life of the country, while their advisory opinions are the source of some important legislative or administrative measures.

§1. The People's Advocate Institution (Ombudsman)

142. The institution of the Ombudsman was first introduced by the Constitution of 1991 under the name of the 'People's Advocate Institution'. It has no tradition in Romania.

According to Article 58 of the Constitution of 2003, the People's Advocate Institution is appointed by both Chambers of the Parliament in a joint session for a term of office of five years, which can be extended only once. In order to qualify for appointment as the People's Advocate Institution, a person should meet the same requirements as one should for becoming a judge for the Constitutional Court and must be a Romanian citizen.

The People's Advocate Institution and its deputies cannot perform any other public or private office, except for teaching positions in higher education.

In terms of exercise of powers, Article 59 provides that the People's Advocate Institution exercises its powers ex officio or on request by persons aggrieved in their rights and freedoms, within the limits established by law. In the exercise of its powers, the People's Advocate Institution is entitled to all necessary support from the public authorities. The People's Advocate Institution has the duty to submit annual reports to Parliament, at the request of the Chambers. The report may include recommendations on legislation or measures of any other nature for the defence of the citizens' rights and freedoms.

Articles 58 and 59 of the Constitution, devoted to the People's Advocate Institution, are consonant with the provisions in CFREU under Article 43 – Ombudsman.

143. The Constitution provides that the organization and functioning of the institution of the People's Advocate Institution shall be regulated by an organic law. The initial law on the organization and functioning of the People's Advocate Institution was Law No. 35/1997. In time, it was amended and supplemented by several laws including Law No. 383/2007 on amending and supplementing Article 36 in Law No. 35/1997 on the organization and functioning of the institution of the People's Advocate Institution, and also by Law No. 258/2010 on amending and supplementing Law No. 35/1997 on the organization and functioning of the institution of the People's Advocate Institution.

At the same time, in April 2002, the Standing Bureaus of the two Chambers of Parliament approved the Regulations on the Organization and Functioning of the People's Advocate Institution. The Regulations lay down the organizational structure, the powers of the special compartments, the legal proceedings for admitting and solving the applications, and the status and disciplinary responsibility of the staff.

Thus, the People's Advocate Institution is an autonomous and independent public authority with respect to any other public authority and aims to protect the rights and freedoms of individuals in their relations with public authorities.

The main duties of the People's Advocate Institution:

- the activity of resolving petitions;
- the activity regarding constitutional disputes:
- drafts points of view, at the request of the Constitutional Court;
- may notify the Constitutional Court regarding the unconstitutionality of laws, before their promulgation;
- may directly notify the Constitutional Court with the exception of unconstitutionality of laws and ordinances;
- the activity regarding administrative disputes: may notify the administrative disputes court, under the terms of the administrative disputes law;
- promoting appeals in the interest of the law before the High Court of Cassation and Justice, regarding legal issues that have been resolved differently by the courts, through irrevocable court decisions;
- presents reports to the two Chambers of Parliament, annually or at their request; the reports may contain recommendations regarding the amendment of legislation or other measures to protect the rights and freedoms of citizens;
- presents reports to the presidents of the two Chambers of Parliament or, as the case may be, to the Prime Minister, in cases where, during the investigations undertaken, he/she finds gaps in legislation or serious cases of corruption or non-compliance with the laws of the country.

The People's Advocate may be consulted by the initiators of draft laws and ordinances, which, through the content of the regulations, concern the rights and freedoms of citizens, provided for by the Constitution of Romania, by the pacts and other international treaties regarding fundamental human rights, to which Romania is a party.

The People's Advocate exercises its powers:

- ex officio or at the request of: natural persons – regardless of citizenship, age, sex, political affiliation or religious beliefs, commercial companies, associations or other legal entities.

While exercising the powers relating to the internal activity of the institution, the People's Advocate Institution issues orders, instructions, methodological rules and regulations.

While exercising the powers relating to the internal activity of the institution, the People's Advocate issues orders, instructions, methodological rules and regulations.

In his activity, the People's Advocate is assisted by deputies. They are appointed for a five-year term by the Standing bureaus of the Deputy Chamber and the Senate, based on a proposal of the People's Advocate, and based on the advise of the juridical commissions of the parliamentary Chambers. They must be university graduate in the fields of Law, Administrative Sciences, Political Sciences, Economics, and Humanities, they must have a eight-year activity in these fields or have been a Senator or Deputy during at least one mandate. The Deputies of the People's Advocate are specialized in the following areas:

- Human rights, gender equality, religious cults and national minorities.
- Family rights, rights of young people, rights of retired people, rights of people with disabilities.
- Defence, protection and promotion of children's rights – the child's advocate.
- Army, justice, police forces, penitentiaries.
- Work, property, social protection, taxes and duties.

According to the law, the People's Advocate Institution presently has the following territorial offices: Alba-Iulia, Bacău, Braşov, Cluj-Napoca, Constanţa, Craiova, Galaţi, Iaşi, Oradea, Piteşti, Ploieşti, Slobozia, Suceava, Târgu-Mureş and Timişoara and the following zonal centres: Bucharest, Alba, Bacău and Craiova.

The staff of the People's Advocate Institution enjoys all the rights applicable to public servants and the immunities applicable to all members of the judiciary.

While performing their duties, the staff of the institution must act with professionalism, loyalty, and fairness, and must promptly and continuously improve their professional training.

§2. The Romanian Institute for Human Rights

144. The Romanian Institute for Human Rights (RIHR), an independent body with legal personality established by law – Law No. 9/1991, is the first national human rights institution created in Romania after 1989 and the only national institution in our country that has been recognized as having this quality by the Coordination Committee of National Institutions for Human Rights of the United Nations (UN) system. The Institute is also a member of the European Network of National Human Rights Institutions, the Association of Francophone Human Rights Commissions, the European Law Institute in Vienna and the International Institute of Law of French Expression and Inspiration.

In its entire activity, the RIHR complied with the Principles of Paris, stated in 1991 at the Conference devoted to national human rights institutions, which later became an official document of the UN General Assembly in 1993. The principles refer to: an 'as broad a mandate as possible' that should be based on the universal standards of human rights and include the double responsibility to promote and protect human rights, while covering all the rights; independence from the Government; independence guaranteed by the Constitution or by the law; adequate power of investigation; pluralism, including the structure of the personnel and/or effective cooperation and adequate human and financial resources. At the same time, the

Institute also evolved in compliance with the requirements laid down by the Council of Europe in its Recommendations R (79) 16 and (97) and Resolution (97) 11 of the Council of Europe Committee of Ministers.

Focusing its preoccupations on the actual realities of each time period, each stage, the Institute had permanently in mind the organization of an adequate framework and the creation of adequate means for the effective application and observance of human rights, for better familiarization with and awareness of these rights, both by public institutions and by natural persons, so much more so that Romania is a member country of the United Nations Organization (UNO), the Organization for Security and Cooperation in Europe (former CSCE – Conference for Security in Europe), the Council of Europe and the EU.

As always, the Institute's mission was considered to be that of acting as an important player so that the fundamental rights should become a reality for all, both in Romania and at European level. Under the circumstances, the Institute focused its activity, laying particular emphasis on programmes and partnerships that best fit the international and the national requirements concerning the promotion of human rights and fundamental freedoms, the training of persons responsible for the protection thereof.

Collaboration with public institutions the academic community, non-governmental bodies concerned with human rights, etc., and the experience accumulated in time provided the Institute with increased capacity to take action in its efforts to fulfil the powers conferred by Law No. 9/1991, in its capacity as national independent institution promoting human rights, to act as an interface, a bridge between these public institutions and the civil society.

The Institute's activity was rewarded in time with a number of international and national prizes awarded by such institutions as the French National Consultative Commission on Human Rights, the Union of Jurists of Romania, and the Mediation Council. In 2015, on occasion of the UN's seventieth anniversary, the Romanian Association for the UN awarded the Institute the Outstanding Merit Award for the promotion of the ideals laid down in the Universal Declaration of Human Rights.

One of the Institute's tasks is to provide a better knowledge to public bodies, non-governmental organizations and the Romanian citizens, of human rights issues and of the way these rights are guaranteed in other countries, particularly in the countries participating in the Conference for Security and Cooperation in Europe. At the same time, the Institute has to inform the public abroad and international bodies about the practical implementation of human rights in Romania. Other purposes of the RIHR are to:

1. cooperate with institutes for human rights and similar bodies in other countries, as well as with international and regional organizations with activities in the field of human rights;
2. educate the citizens, particularly the younger generation, in the field of human rights;
3. creation, maintain and run to the benefit of all users the Documentation Centre in the field of human rights, supplying: texts of international conventions, laws, documents, studies and publications, reference books;

4. keep informed public bodies, non-governmental organizations, citizens, mainly by acquainting them with the international documents, practice and methodology in the field of human rights;
5. provide, on request or regularly, information about the activities undertaken at the governmental and non-governmental level in Romania to promote and protect human rights, as well as about similar activities in other countries and about the international commitments of Romania and the way they are brought into effect; and
6. provide documentation requested by the parliamentary commissions on aspects related to human rights in draft laws and other issues considered by the Parliament.

145. The Institute's teaching and training activities mainly consist of:

1. organization and training programmes especially meant for those categories of persons, specific responsibilities for the protection of human rights or the dissemination of knowledge about human rights among large segments of population (lawyers, police, teaching staff, workers in the field of social assistance and protection, etc.);
2. assistance, by involving highly qualified specialists, for the organization of lectures on human rights in the main higher education institutions in Romania; and
3. invitation of political personalities from various countries, specialists well known for their activities of worldwide promotion of human rights, for courses of lectures organized by the Romanian universities.

146. The Institute also performs an important research activity in the field of human rights. The research, which is devoted to various aspects related to the promotion and observance of human rights in Romania and at international level, may be carried out by the Institute's staff or as a result of contracts with science institutions and bodies.

147. The RIHR also has an intensive publishing activity. This activity mainly consists of:

1. editing of a periodical entitled 'Human Rights', where the following are published:
   a. texts of international conventions, laws, documents, and other international regulations on human rights;
   b. studies by the Institute, as well as international studies in the field of human rights;
   c. bibliographies;
   d. studies on comparative law;
   e. inquiries, roundtables, opinions by Romanian or international personalities and people dealing in practice with particular issues in the field of human rights; and

f. information about the activities of governmental and non-governmental institutions concerned with human rights;

2. publication of folders, booklets, teaching material, mainly methodological in nature, including textbooks on human rights to be used in schools and higher education institutes; and
3. organization and publication of statistical data resulting from inquiries on different aspects concerning the protection of human rights in Romania.

§3. National Council for Combating Discrimination

148. The National Council for Combating Discrimination was established and is functioning under Government Decision No. 1194/2001, with its subsequent amendments and supplementations. It is an autonomous public authority, under parliamentary control, whose activity is focused on discrimination. The Council guarantees respect and implementation of the principle of non-discrimination, in conformity with the domestic legislation and the international documents where Romania is a party.

§4. The Department for Inter-ethnic Relations

149. The Department for Inter-ethnic Relations is an entity that does not have the status of a legal person, organized and functioning on the basis of Government Decision No. 111/2005. It is subordinated to the Prime Minister and coordinated by the Delegate Minister in charge with the coordination of the Government Secretariat General. According to the legal provisions, its main competencies include to:

1. implement the policy established under the Governing Programme in the field of inter-ethnic relationships;
2. elaborate strategies and policies for the preservation, advancement and development of the ethnic identity of persons belonging to national minorities and submit them to the Government for approval;
3. elaborate drafts of laws and other normative acts in its field of activity;
4. endorse drafts of laws and other normative acts that have an impact upon the rights and the duties of persons belonging to national minorities;
5. monitor the application of the domestic and international normative acts related to the protection of national minorities;
6. participate in the elaboration of the Report on Romania's implementation of the Framework Convention for the Protection of National Minorities adopted by the Council of Europe, as well as to elaborate the chapters referring to national minorities in Romania's reports submitted to other international institutions and bodies;
7. stimulate the majority – national minorities dialogue in order to improve the decision-making process and the implementation measures;

8. cultivate the common values, to combat discrimination and prejudices by promoting cultural, linguistic and confessional diversity through activities performed in the framework of various projects;
9. promote and organize programmes meant to guarantee, preserve, express, promote and develop the ethnic, cultural, linguistic and religious identity of persons belonging to national minorities; and
10. assist the achievement of inter-ethnic programmes or activities initiated by organizations, associations, foundations or public institutions, etc.

At the same time, the Department maintains collaboration relationships with the *Council of National Minorities*, which it coordinates. The Council of National Minorities is made up of three representatives of each organization of the citizens belonging to the national minorities that are represented in Parliament.

Another entity coordinated by the Department for Inter-ethnic Relations is the *Romanian Institute for Research on National Minorities*, established by Government Ordinance No. 121/2000 and functioning in accordance with Government Decree No. 893/2007. The purpose of this institute is to conduct inter- and multidisciplinary studies and research with regard to the preservation, development and expression of ethnic identity, as well as about social, historical, cultural, linguistic, religious or other aspects of national minorities and of other ethnic communities living in Romania.

Part III. Organization of the State

§1. Organization of the State

150. As was shown earlier in this presentation, Romania is a sovereign, independent, unitary and indivisible State. Its form is that of a republic based on such principles as: the national character of the State; State sovereignty; the unitary and indivisible character of the State; the rule of law principle; the democratic and social character of the State; and constitutional democracy.

Romania's historical provinces, which were mentioned in the introductory part of this study, have no administrative relevance.

I. Decentralized Authorities

151. The Constitution proclaims, in its Article 1, that Romania's territory is inalienable. The territory is organized administratively into communes, towns and counties. Some towns are declared municipalities, according to the provisions of the law.

The constitutional principle of local autonomy was enshrined, before the present Administrative Code[91] came into force, within Law No. 215 of 23 April 2001, the Public Administration Act, with its subsequent amendments and supplementations.[92]

The principles governing the public administration are, according to the Administrative Code: the principle of legality, the principle of equity, the principle of transparency, the principle of proportionality, meeting the public interest, the principle of impartiality, and the principle of adaptability. We should like to mention the Code has modified previous legislation in order to develop and improve local public services.

91. The Emergency Ordinance No. 57/3.7.2019 on the Administrative Code was published in the Monitorul Oficial, Part I, No. 555/5.7.2019. *See* Verginia Vedinas, Codul Administrativ adnotat. Noutati. Examinare comparative. Note explicative. editia a III-a, revazuta si adaugita, Bucureşti, Editura Universul Juridic, 2021, pp. 7 and the following. We would like to mention that, before the Code, the National Decentralization Strategy had been adopted, by Government Decision 229/12.4.2017.
92. This Law was abolished once the Emergency Ordinance No. 57/2019 was published, except for a few articles that were abolished later on, on the date the local elections took place in 2020.

The above-mentioned amendments testify to the Government's commitment concerning the reforming of public administration, which mainly aims to continue the administrative and financial decentralization, the increase of local autonomy being an important step.

The principles governing public administration in territorial-administrative units are the general ones, stipulated within Part.I Title III within the Administrative Code and those stipulated within Law No. 199/1997, as well as the specific ones: decentralization, local autonomy, eligibility of the local public administration authorities, liability, cooperation, consultation of the citizens' opinions on local matters of particular interest, and budget limitation.

The legislator provides that local autonomy shall be only administrative and financial being exercised on the basis and within the limits of the law, while stipulating that local autonomy regards such issues as organization, competencies, powers as well as management of the resources which, according to the law, belong to the commune, town, municipality or county, as the case may be.

One of the most important provisions states that by no means can the application of the above-mentioned principles undermine Romania's capacity as a national, unitary and indivisible State. Thus, the constitutional concept of local autonomy comes to life.

152. The administrative-territorial units are the communes, the towns, the municipalities and the counties. Communes – the smallest unit – are formed of one or several villages and hamlets. Some towns – those that meet certain conditions provided for by the law – can be declared municipalities. The latter can have administrative-territorial subdivisions, whose organization and delimitation shall be stipulated by the law. Thus, the municipality of Bucharest is divided into six sectors.

A most important provision is that all administrative-territorial units (local public administration) are autonomous structures, whether elected or appointed at the local level, which manage public affairs in administrative territorial units (municipalities, cities, counties), having legal personality and their own budget, distinct from the central ones. They hold the initiative in everything related to the administration of local public interests, exerting authority, under the law, within the established territorial limits. As civil legal persons, they own private assets, while as legal persons under public law, they are owners of the local assets of the public domain.

There are several authorities through which local autonomy is achieved (Article 3 of the Administrative Code) – Local Councils, Mayors, County Councils and their presidents, in their capacity as authorities of the local public administration elected through universal, equal, direct, secret and freely expressed vote. Such authorities can also be instituted for the administrative-territorial units of municipalities, which are then subordinated to the respective administrative authorities of the municipalities. The law provides that the Local Councils and the Mayors' offices operate as autonomous administrative authorities.

As far as counties are concerned, there is a County Council that coordinates the activity of the local councils in order to have the public services performed and elects, from among its members, a president and a number of county counsellors.

The number of the County Council's members is established by a Prefect's order based on the number of inhabitants in the respective county.

153. An exceptional importance is attached to the relationships between local authorities. Thus, the relationships between the county and the local public administration shall be based on the principles of autonomy, legality and cooperation in addressing the common problems. There shall be no subordination in the relationship between the local and the county administration.

According to the requirements of local autonomy, the public administration authorities in communes, towns and counties have their own revenue and expenditure budgets which they themselves approve, and they are entitled to institute and collect local taxes and duties, as provided by the law. The law provides that the local bodies may decide to organize a local referendum in relation to problems of particular local interest.

154. The Government appoints a Prefect for every county and for the municipality of Bucharest. He shall be the representative of the Government and coordinate and supervise the public services fulfilled by the ministries and the other central administration authorities, organized in the administrative-territorial units.

Even though the Prefect has no decision or control power in relation to the activity of the local bodies, he is however authorized by the law to attack the acts thereof before the administrative court, in case he deems they are illegal. The law provides that the act against which proceedings were thus instituted shall be suspended de jure.

155. Communes, towns and municipalities have an elected Mayor, while the municipality of Bucharest has a Mayor General. Each sector of Bucharest has its own Mayor.

The Mayor participates, de jure, in the Local Council sessions, but he is not the president of this council. According to the law, the Mayor – as well as the Mayor General of the Capital – are the heads of the local public administration and shall be responsible before the Local Council for its activity. The Mayor shall represent the commune or the town in the relations with the natural or legal persons from the country and from abroad, as well as in court. In the exercise of his powers, the Mayor shall issue decisions that become enforceable after having been announced to the persons involved.

II. The Romanian Citizenship

156. Article 5 of the Constitution of Romania provides that Romanian citizenship can be acquired or lost as provided by an organic law. It is also provided that Romanian citizenship cannot be withdrawn if acquired by birth.

Acquisition and loss of Romanian citizenship are regulated by the Romanian Citizenship Act (Law No. 21 of 1 March 1991), amended and supplemented.[93]

According to the Romanian Citizenship Act, Romanian citizenship can be acquired by birth, adoption, repatriation, and on request.

157. The first way to acquire Romanian citizenship is, therefore, by birth. Children born on the territory of Romania, one or both of whose parents are Romanian citizens, shall be Romanian citizens. Likewise, children born abroad, one or both of whose parents are Romanian, shall be Romanian citizens. Also, a child found on the territory of Romania, whose parents are both unknown, shall be a Romanian citizen.

158. The second way Romanian citizenship can be acquired is adoption, provided that the adopters are Romanian citizens and the adopted child has not reached the age of 18. The new Civil Code[94] provides for the possibility to adopt persons who have reached the age of 18, provided that they were raised by the adopters. However, they do not acquire Romanian citizenship. If one of the adopters is a Romanian citizen, the citizenship of the adopted juvenile shall be decided by mutual agreement between the adopters. In case they do not agree, the matter shall be submitted to the court of law, which has to decide while taking into account the interests of the juvenile. A child who has reached the age of 14 shall be asked for consent.

According to the Romanian law, it is possible for adoption to be made by one person only. In that case, if the adopter is a Romanian citizen, the juvenile shall acquire his citizenship.

In case adoption is nullified or annulled, the child who has not reached the age of 18 is considered to have never been a Romanian citizen, if he lives abroad or leaves the country in order to live abroad. *Per a contrario,* if the juvenile continues to live in Romania, he keeps the Romanian citizenship, for the retroactive effect of the annulment does not affect it.

159. As was mentioned above, regaining is another way to acquire Romanian citizenship.[95] A person who has lost Romanian citizenship may regain it (also descendants up to second degree), while keeping another citizenship. Parents shall decide for their juvenile children. If they do not agree, the tribunal within whose jurisdiction the juvenile's domicile is shall decide, taking into account the child's interests and, if the child has reached the age of 14, with his consent. As in the case of adoption, the Romanian law here takes into account the International Convention on the Rights of the Child.

---

93. Republished (r2) in Monitorul Oficial, Part I, No. 576/13.8.2019, consolidated on 11 April 2023. *See also* the Emergency Ordinance No. 5/2010 on the establishment, organization and functioning of the National Authority for Citizenship.
94. The new Civil Code was adopted in 2011.
95. In regard of costs for repatriation of deceased Romanian citizens, *see* Law No. 270/1.11.2024 published in Monitorul Oficial Part I, No. 1099/4.11.2024 and EGO 156/30.12.2024 published in Monitorul Oficial Part.I, No. 1334/31.12.2024.

Regaining of citizenship by one of the spouses has no consequences for the other spouse who, if a foreign citizen, may apply for Romanian citizenship under the conditions provided for by the law.

160. Finally, Romanian citizenship may be granted on request by a foreign citizen or a person having no citizenship (naturalization) who:

1. was born in Romania and is living on Romania's territory on the date of the application, or, although not born in Romania, has been living in Romania for at least eight years or has been married to and lives with a Romanian citizen for at least five years;
2. proves, by behaviour and attitude, his attachment towards the Romanian State and people;
3. has reached the age of 18;
4. has the legal means to make a living;
5. is known to have a good conduct and was not convicted, in Romania or abroad, for a crime that makes him unworthy of Romanian citizenship; and
6. commands the Romanian language/culture well enough for social integration.

Under well-justified circumstances, the time periods provided under (1) can be reduced by up to half.

The child born of foreign parents or whose parents have no citizenship and who has not reached the age of 18 shall be granted Romanian citizenship at the same time as the parents.

In case only one parent acquires the Romanian citizenship, the parents shall decide, by mutual agreement, as to their child's citizenship; in case they cannot reach an agreement, the disagreement shall be brought before the tribunal in whose jurisdiction the child's domicile is, and the tribunal shall make the decision. Consent of the child who has reached the age of 14 is necessary. In all cases, the child shall acquire citizenship at the same time as the parents.

According to the law, Romanian citizenship can be regained by those who lost it, provided they meet the conditions listed above under (2), (3) and (5).

161. As far as the procedure is concerned, a Board of Citizenship has to be established. The Board of Citizenship, also referred to as the Commission, is an entity without legal personality operating within the National Citizenship Authority. The Board first has to check whether the conditions provided in the law are met for the granting, reacquisition, withdrawal or renunciation of Romanian citizenship.

The Board includes a technical secretariat set up within the National Citizenship Authority.

The members and the chair of the Board are appointed by order of the Minister of Justice for a term of two years and they may be revoked throughout the duration of their term by means of an order issued by the Minister of Justice.

The Board's activity is permanent. It is composed of a chairperson and twenty members, who are members of the personnel of the National Citizenship Authority. The work of the Board is not public, and it may take place only in the presence of at least three members. The Board is presided over by the chairperson and in his absence by a member that the chairperson has designated.

162. The fulfilment or, where appropriate, the failure to fulfil the legal requirements for the acquisition or reacquisition of Romanian citizenship is recorded in an argued report which is subject to adoption by the Board with the vote of the majority of those present. In the event of parity, the vote of the chair of the Board or of his replacement shall be decisive.

The application for acquiring or reacquiring Romanian citizenship is registered with the technical secretariat of the Board. If it is found that documents are missing which are required in order to process the application, the chair of the Board issues a resolution requesting that the record be supplemented. If the required documents are not sent within six months from receipt of the request, the application shall be dismissed on grounds of lack of supporting documents.

The chair of the Board shall issue a resolution to appoint the hearing date when the debates regarding the application will take place.

At the date appointed for hearing the application, the Board shall check whether the requirements are met for the acquisition or reacquisition of citizenship.

If it finds it necessary to hear persons who could provide useful information for processing the application, the Board may order that they be summoned and appoint a new hearing date.

163. In the event that the requirements are met for granting Romanian citizenship, the Board shall make, within a time limit not exceeding six months, an appointment for the person concerned.

The chair of the Board of Citizenship shall, by means of orders:

1. request information from any authority about the fulfilment of the requirements;
2. request additional supporting documents, within no more than two months from receipt by the applicant of the request by the technical secretariat of the Board; and
3. appoint the date when the Board will check the fulfilment of the requirements for acquisition or reacquisition of Romanian citizenship, a date which must be within five months of the date when the application was registered.

If the legal requirements are not met for acquisition or reacquisition of Romanian citizenship, and also in the event of failure in the interview or unjustified failure to appear for the interview, the Board shall, in an argued report, propose to the chairperson of the National Citizenship Authority the dismissal of the application.

A new application for acquisition or reacquisition of Romanian citizenship may be submitted after six months from the dismissal of the previous application.

If the applicant succeeds in the interview, the Board shall draw up a report mentioning the fulfilment of legal requirements for the acquisition or, where appropriate, reacquisition of citizenship. The report, together with the application for acquisition or reacquisition of citizenship, shall be forwarded to the chairperson of the National Citizenship Authority.

The chairperson of the National Citizenship Authority shall, after finding that the legal requirements are met, issue the order of acquisition or reacquisition of Romanian citizenship, as appropriate. The order of acquisition or reacquisition of Romanian citizenship shall be served on the applicant, by means of registered letter with acknowledgement of receipt, at once, from the date when the order is issued.

If he finds that the legal requirements are not met, the chairperson of the National Citizenship Authority shall dismiss the application for acquisition or reacquisition of Romanian citizenship by means of an order.

164. The order by the chairperson of the National Citizenship Authority regarding the acquisition or reacquisition of Romanian citizenship, and respectively the order of dismissal of the application for acquisition or reacquisition of Romanian citizenship, shall be communicated at once to the applicant, by registered post with acknowledgement of receipt.

The order of dismissal of the application for acquisition or reacquisition of Romanian citizenship may be appealed, within fifteen days from service, to the Court of Appeal of Bucharest, section for administrative disputed claims. The decision by the Court of Appeal shall be final and may be subject to appeal on points of law at the Administrative Disputed Claims of the High Court of Cassation and Justice.

165. Romanian citizenship is acquired or re-acquired on the date when the oath of loyalty is taken. Within three months from the date of service of the order by the chairperson of the National Citizenship Authority regarding the acquisition or reacquisition of Romanian citizenship, the persons who have acquired or reacquired Romanian citizenship shall take an oath of loyalty to Romania. The oath of loyalty is taken in a solemn session before the Minister of Justice and the chairperson of the National Citizenship Authority or one of the two deputy chairpersons of the authority who have been delegated for that purpose.

After the oath is taken, the Board shall issue the certificate of Romanian citizenship, which shall be drawn up in two originals, signed by the chairperson of the National Citizenship Authority. One of the originals must be handed to the holder thereof. Both originals of the certificate include safety elements and the photo of the holder.

166. Loss of Romanian citizenship can take place as a result of:

1. withdrawal;
2. approval of an application to give up the Romanian citizenship; and
3. other cases provided for by the law.

Romanian citizenship may be withdrawn from a person who:

1. while abroad, commits particularly grievous acts that are harmful to the interests of the Romanian State or to the prestige of Romania;
2. while abroad, joins the armed forces of a State with which Romania has ceased diplomatic relations or with which Romania is at war;
3. has obtained Romanian citizenship by fraudulent means; and

4. is known to have connections with terrorist groups or to have supported them, in any form, or has committed other acts that are a threat to national security.

Romanian citizenship cannot be withdrawn from a person who has acquired it by birth.

Withdrawal of a person's citizenship cannot have effects upon the citizenship of that person's spouse or children, no matter how the latter have acquired it.

167. For justified reasons, renunciation of Romanian citizenship may be approved for persons aged 18 or older who:

1. do not have the capacity of accused or defendants in criminal proceedings and are not under an obligation to serve any criminal sentence;
2. are not being prosecuted for debt towards the State, towards natural or legal persons in Romania or, while having such debt, pays it or provides appropriate guarantees that it will be paid; and
3. has acquired a different citizenship or has applied to obtain it and has the assurance that he will obtain it.

Loss of Romanian citizenship by approval of renunciation shall not take any effect upon the citizenship of the spouse or minor children.

Nevertheless, in the event that both parents obtain an approval of renunciation of Romanian citizenship, and their minor child is abroad with them or leaves Romania together with them, the minor child shall lose Romanian citizenship together with his parents, and if they have lost it at different dates, the minor child shall lose it at the last of those dates. The minor child who, in order to domicile abroad, leaves Romania after both parents have lost Romanian citizenship shall lose Romanian citizenship on the date when he leaves Romania.

This shall also apply where only one of the parents is known or is alive.

A minor child whose custody has been awarded by a court judgment to the parent who is domiciled abroad and who renounced citizenship shall lose Romanian citizenship on the same date as the parent who has custody of him and with whom he is living, on condition that the consent is obtained of the other parent, who is a Romanian citizen.

The consent of children who have reached the age of 14 must be obtained.

168. Other cases of loss of Romanian citizenship are:

1. A minor child who is a Romanian citizen and has been adopted by a foreign citizen shall lose Romanian citizenship if, at the request of his adopter(s), he has acquired their citizenship under foreign law. The consent of children who have reached the age of 14 must be obtained.
2. The date when Romanian citizenship is lost shall be the date when the minor child obtains the citizenship of his adopter.
3. If adoption is declared null or is cancelled, children below the age of 18 shall be regarded as never having lost Romanian citizenship.

4. In the case of found children whose parents are unknown, the respective children shall lose Romanian citizenship if by the age of 18 their filiation has been established regarding both parents and they are foreign citizens.
5. Romanian citizenship shall also be lost if filiation has been established only regarding one parent who is a foreign citizen and the other parent remains unknown.

The date when Romanian citizenship is lost shall be the date when the child's filiation is established.

For withdrawal of the citizenship or approval of giving up the citizenship, the law provides for a procedure symmetrical to that of the granting of citizenship, the decision being made by order of the chairperson of the National Citizenship Authority.

Romanian citizenship is required for the enjoyment of political rights, the right to hold a public office or dignity, and the right to possess land. It does not, however, influence basic human rights, which are equally guaranteed to all persons on Romanian territory.

Part IV. Specific Problems

§1. Fundamental Rights and Freedoms

169. Once communist totalitarianism was overthrown, and the assertion of the ideals of a democratic and free society was made, the role and the place of the citizen within the general framework of the country's political, economic, social and cultural structures were reconsidered. In this respect, paragraph 3 of Article 1 proclaims that human dignity, the citizens' rights and freedoms, the free development of human personality, justice and political pluralism represent supreme values and shall be guaranteed.

The Constitution deals with the fundamental rights, freedoms and obligations in its Title II. It is an expression of the new concept according to which the citizen, with his requirements as an individual and as member of a group, represents the central element of the constitutional construction. The State must be in the service of the citizen; self-limitation of the power of public authorities and the provision of effectiveness of human rights and freedoms are basic features of the system. Likewise, the declaration of rights protected by the Constitution has assimilated the international standards on human rights, particularly those of the Universal Declaration of Human Rights and of the international covenants,[96] as well as the declarations of rights in the constitutions of other democratic countries, especially the European ones, including Romania's Constitution of 1923.

170. There are several principles governing the constitutional conception of the citizens' fundamental human rights.

Universality, provided for by paragraph 1 of Article 15, means that the rights and freedoms are recognized by all and are indivisible, as they originate in the dignity of the person. They are thus imposed on the State as well as on any other subject. Since they are universal, no one can be excluded from the exercise thereof, while at the same time, they offer the citizens equal chances, as well as the means and the safeguards to achieve them.

171. Equality of rights is provided for by Article 16 of the Constitution. According to this principle, citizens are equally treated, without any privileges or discrimination, by both public authorities and any other subjects, whether natural or juridical persons, irrespective of their nationality, ethnic origin, language, religion, sex,

96. Victor Dan Zlătescu and Irina Moroianu Zlătescu, *Human Rights in Action* (Editura IRDO, Bucureşti, 1993), pp. 3ff.

political opinion or adherence, and economic, social and cultural status. The main aspects of equality of the citizens before the law refer to non-discrimination between the sexes, interdiction of any discrimination on such grounds as race, nationality or ethnic origin, language, possessions or social origin, and equality in rights irrespective of religion, political opinion or adherence.

Provisions of Article 16 in the Constitution of Romania are also to be found in such international human rights instruments as the CFREU in its Articles 20 (Equality before the law) and 23 (equality between men and women) and the European Social Charter Revised (ESCR) in its Articles 20 (The right to equal opportunities and equal treatment in matters of employment and occupation without discrimination on the grounds of sex) and 27 (the right of workers with family responsibilities to equal opportunities and equal treatment).

Application of the principle of equality of rights is the reason why the Constitution provides for a system of protecting measures for the preservation, development and expression of the identity of persons belonging to national minorities, and the implementation of certain protection rules for disadvantaged social categories or for the benefit of certain categories, such as children, the young, the handicapped, etc. Such protections are not considered discriminatory; on the contrary, they are meant to guarantee, as much as possible, the effectiveness of citizens' equality. A corollary of citizens' equality before the law is the principle provided by paragraph 2 of Article 16, according to which no one is above the law, the immunities and privileges granted to certain persons during the communist regime in terms of their political status being thereby forbidden.

There is, nevertheless, an exception to the principle of equality. This exception is provided by Article 16 paragraph 3, according to which access to a public office or dignity is granted to persons whose citizenship is only and exclusively Romanian, and whose domicile is in Romania. This excludes citizens with dual citizenship or citizens whose domicile is abroad. It is the consequence of the fact that a person, however impartial and objective, cannot promote, in the exercise of a public office or dignity, the national interests of several States. Cumulative fidelity towards different countries is impossible, especially in the light of Article 54 of the Constitution which, referring to citizens holding a public office, provides that they are liable for the loyal fulfilment of the obligations they are bound to and shall, for this purpose, take the oath as requested by law.

172. The principle of *precedence of the international regulations on human rights* is laid down in Article 20 of the Constitution. It is the logical consequence of a fundamental view of the Constituent Assembly regarding the international standards on human rights and has a triple significance.

First, it is a consecration of the monistic principle in perceiving international law. According to Article 11, paragraph 2 of the Constitution, treaties ratified by Parliament according to the law are part of national law. Unity of public law is therefore ensured on the basis of precedence of international regulations. This eliminated the dualistic principle that had previously existed and whose effects were unavoidable disagreement, at least for a period of time, between international norms and internal ones as a result of the shield of the law in the reception of the international norm.

Second, it is a consecration of the precedence given to the interpretation of international norms in the field of human rights in applying the corresponding national legal provisions, constitutional or of a different nature. In this respect, paragraph 1 of Article 20 provides that the constitutional provisions concerning the citizens' rights and liberties shall be interpreted and enforced in conformity with the Universal Declaration of Human Rights and with the covenants and other treaties Romania is a party to. Thus, the Universal Declaration, which was not adopted as an international convention, received within Romanian law the value of a constitutional norm. It is applicable law, of course, to the extent its provisions are to be found in an internal legal provision, which, nevertheless, is not an obstacle since the constitutional declaration of rights and freedoms implies such an agreement.

Finally, precedence of the international regulations that conflict with an internal regulation (paragraph 2 of Article 20) is a principle that ensures dynamism in the development of internal law in terms of international developments in the field of human rights, integration of the internal law with the international one, and their unity as an expression of the unity of public law. After all, the principle we are referring to is the consequence of the two above-mentioned principles and the final conclusion of the monistic conception of the Constituent Assembly. There is, however, an exception to this principle: those cases where the Constitution or national laws comprise more favourable provisions.[97]

173. The principle of *non-retroactivity of the law* was included in the Constitution, on the one hand, as a result of the reaction of the Constituent Assembly to the communist practice of retroactive application of the law, even to incriminate certain deeds. On the other hand, it is the expression of a broader conception aiming to ensure, as much as possible, stability of the acquired rights as well as of the constitutional protection of freedom and personal security. This principle, provided by Article 15 paragraph 2, has just one exception that refers to the retroactive adoption of a more favourable criminal law.

As regards interpretative laws, these obviously are confined to clarifying the meaning of the interpreted norm and, therefore, neither add nor modify anything. Since an interpretative law only clarifies an existing law in terms of the diversity of situations covered by the norm, such a law does not represent an exception to the non-retroactivity of the law. It is the lawmaker's duty to produce clear laws, a duty which, if not fulfilled from the beginning, still can be fulfilled later.

174. The principle of a *special protection of the citizens.* Starting with the fact the Romanian citizenship is the juridical and political link between the State and the citizens which determines their status, wherever they be, within or beyond the country's frontiers, Article 17 of the Constitution provides that the State shall provide protection for Romanian citizens when they are abroad, while the citizens are only exempted from those obligations that are incompatible with their absence from the

97. The exception referring to the application of the most favourable legal provision was added in the revised text of 2003.

country. It appears from the constitutional text that, on the contrary, their rights cannot be affected by their absence. Also included among the special protection measures is the rule provided by Article 19, according to which a Romanian citizen may not be extradited or expelled from Romania. This is the consequence of the constitutional protection of certain specific rights, namely personal freedom and the right to free movement, as well as the citizenship link that obliges the State to protect all its citizens. Likewise, the rule provided by Article 5 paragraph 2 is that Romanian citizenship cannot be withdrawn if acquired by birth.

175. The principle of the *protection of aliens*. Aliens and stateless persons living in Romania shall enjoy general protection of their person and assets, as guaranteed by the Constitution and other laws. Essentially, in comparison to Romanian citizens, they do not enjoy those rights that are the exclusive prerogatives of Romanian citizens, namely, political rights, the right to hold a public office or dignity – which does not exclude carrying out services, on a contractual basis, for the benefit of a public authority – and the right to possess land. However, the fundamental rights that belong to the category of human rights – that is, inherent to human beings – are also to be enjoyed by aliens, citizens of another state or stateless persons.

176. There are certain instances when the general interests of the country impose certain restrictions on the fundamental rights and freedoms. According to the Constitution, the exercise of the fundamental rights and freedoms can be limited, but only under those exceptional circumstances listed by the Constitution. In this respect, Article 53 provides that the exercise of certain rights or freedoms may be restricted only by law, and only if absolutely unavoidable for: the defence of national security, public order, health or morals, or the citizens' rights and freedoms; conducting a criminal investigation; or the prevention of the consequences of a natural calamity or extremely grave disaster.

The second paragraph of this Article lays down two basic principles.

The principle of *proportionality*. In this respect, the constitutional text provides that the restriction shall be proportional to the extent of the situation that requires it.

The principle of the *supremacy of law* is illustrated by the provision that the restriction may not infringe upon the existence of the respective right or freedom.

It is important to mention that, according to Article 152 of the Constitution, no revision thereof shall be made if it results in the suppression of the citizens' fundamental rights and freedoms, or the safeguards thereof.

177. It comes out that any limitation of the fundamental rights should be done in accordance with the following principles:

1. *the citizens' fundamental rights and freedoms cannot be suppressed*, not even by revision of the Constitution, and therefore enjoy, within their constitutional limits, a certain supremacy as their respect is imposed on all authorities, the lawmaker included, even as a derived constitutional power;

2. by virtue of their supremacy, *the exercise of the fundamental rights and freedoms cannot be suspended*, paragraph 2 of Article 53 providing in this respect that the restriction may not infringe upon the existence of the respective right or freedom;
3. *restriction of the exercise is only allowed in those limited cases provided for by paragraph 1 of Article 53* which, basically, concerns motives of public order qualified by the Constitution itself; that is why consideration by the lawmaker of the enforcement of such restrictions is exclusively permitted within the limits thus defined; and
4. the restriction is only permitted through the law. No other authority besides the lawmaker may restrict the exercise of a right or freedom. Taking into consideration the classification of laws into organic and common, as well as the derogatory character of the rights-restricting law, it follows that this law should also be either organic or common, depending on what kind of law provides for the affected right or freedom.

Many classifications of the fundamental rights and freedoms have been made in time, in both Romania and other countries. Without covering everything, each has the merit of revealing certain aspects.

178. One of these classifications, related to the contents of the rights and freedoms enforced by the Constitution, has the advantage of being close to the classifications used in relation to human rights. According to this classification, which takes into account the contents of the fundamental rights and freedoms, these may be classified into: inviolabilities, exclusively political rights, freedoms of opinion, social-economic and cultural rights and freedoms, and guarantee rights.

179. Inviolabilities include: the right to life; the right to physical integrity; the right to psychological integrity; personal freedom; the right to defence; the right to free circulation; the right to protection of the intimate, family and private life; and inviolability of the domicile. Their basic characteristic feature is that they represent 'target-freedoms' as they provide the beneficiary the possibility to perform an autonomous activity, protected against any imposition. For this reason, they are also negative rights as they imply on the part of the authorities a general obligation of self-restraint. They define a discretionary right of the holder, which is however exercised as provided by the law, i.e., under certain circumstances which, without being restrictions are conditions for their exercise. Such conditions are: the obligation to notify the police about a change of domicile so that the latter can keep population records; formalities related to travelling across borders (passport and visa, if requested, customs formalities, observation of the established border-crossing points); conclusion of the juridical assistance contract by virtue of the right to defence, etc. A much-debated problem is that of freedom of abortion; there is public pressure for the prohibition thereof by virtue of the right to life.

As a rule, the rights grouped under the category of inviolabilities confer on the holder an effective protection, as he has at all times the possibility to address the judiciary for their defence, and it is enough for him to prove the violation of the general obligation of self-restraint by the party who infringed upon his right.

180. Seen from an exclusivist point of view, political rights refer to the right to vote and the right to be elected. They are exercised on the basis of Articles 37 and 38 of the Constitution, according to which the right to vote shall be recognized to those citizens who have attained the age of 18 by or on the election day. This right cannot be enjoyed by mentally deficient persons, alienated persons, persons under interdiction, as well as persons disenfranchised by a final decision of the court. These indignities, having the quality of an exception, are to be strictly interpreted.

Article 37 paragraph 2 lays down the minimum age required for the right to be elected to be enjoyed: at least 23 years for the Chamber of Deputies or the local authorities, at least 33 years for the Senate and at least 35 years for the office of President of Romania. The right to be elected shall be enjoyed by all citizens having the right to vote on the negative condition they do not fall under the ineligibilities provided by paragraph 1 of Article 37, referring to citizens who cannot hold a public office or dignity as they do not have exclusively Romanian citizenship or a domicile in Romania (Article 16 paragraph 3 of the Constitution) or who are forbidden to adhere to political parties as they hold a depoliticized public office according to Article 40 paragraph 3 of the Constitution.

The exercise of these rights is regulated by the Electoral Law, particularly referring to nomination, the voting technique, and the resolution of challenges.

Taking into account that at the time when the constitutional text was revised (2003), Romania was a candidate for accession to the EU, the Constitution of 2003 was introduced a new article, Article 38, according to which once Romania becomes a member country of the EU, Romanian citizens have the right to elect and be elected to the European Parliament.

As far as inviolabilities are concerned, political rights confer on the holders a discretionary right: freedom of suffrage and freedom to be a candidate. However, the exercise of the rights depends on the way the State fulfils its administrative obligations for the organization of free and fair elections. Similarly, nomination depends on the fulfilment of particular requirements related to political pluralism, the support of political parties, and certain representativeness in the case of independent nominations. So the exercise of political rights also implies certain positive actions and not mere self-restraint on the part of the authorities. It therefore has the characteristic features of a claim-right, even if this aspect is subordinated to the essential one related to the target-freedom that represents its hard, defining core, which is expressed by the right of the holder to trigger the challenge procedure in case of dispute.

The constitutional provisions under Articles 36, 37 and 38 related to the electoral rights match certain provisions of CFREU (Article 39 – Right to vote and to stand as a candidate at elections to the European Parliament; Article 40 – Right to vote and to stand as a candidate at municipal elections) and also in First Optional Protocol to the ECHR (ECHR-P1; Article 3 – The right to free elections).

181. Freedom of opinion refers to one's possibility to express personal thoughts and opinions, either when elections are held, or for solving social or spiritual problems, or for participation in government, mainly as a result of the pre-eminence of public opinion in this process. This category includes freedom of conscience, freedom of expression, the right to information, freedom of assembly, right of association, and secrecy of correspondence.

Inviolabilities in particular, but political rights too, generally have an altogether individual character. While this is true, some of the rights belonging to the category of freedoms of opinion can be exercised collectively only, as in the case of the *right of association* or *freedom of assembly*. At the same time, the stronger impact the exercise of these rights has upon the public or the more it implies the use of important public means, the greater the importance of positive action by society and particularly by the State for the fulfilment of these rights. In this respect, for example, we shall mention freedom of the audio-visual media which, when referring to the state-owned radio and television companies, imposes upon them, as well as on the competent public authority – the National Council of the Audio-Visual Media – the obligation to observe a genuine, representative pluralism. The same holds true regarding the security of meetings that is incumbent on the police; numerous examples can be given in this respect. What is essential is that, just like exclusively political rights, these positive actions have a subordinated character, since freedoms of opinion are substantially another target-freedom. They actually represent forms by which freedom of conscience is developed.

182. It is quite obvious that freedom of conscience necessarily implies freedom of expression, including meetings, the right to information and to secrecy of correspondence, as well as the right of association. For this reason, freedoms of opinion give the holder the possibility to take action against the violation of the self-restraint obligation generally related to target-freedoms and also, as provided by the law, the right to complain of failure to carry out the positive action, the exercise thereof depends on. Of course, the action must be sufficiently characterized to outline a sub-adjacent right, such as failure to authorize a meeting in spite of the fact that the requirements for authorization are met, or refusal to register an association before the court even though the form and content criteria were met, etc.

It was shown earlier that freedom of conscience is the basis of the constitutional concept of freedom of opinion. This implies pluralism in its broadest sense. Particularly, three aspects are to be considered: political pluralism which, according to Article 1 paragraph 3 of the Constitution, is proclaimed a supreme value; cultural pluralism, the linguistic, ethnic, ideological, etc. ones included; and religious freedom.

183. In terms of freedom of expression, a special role is played by *freedom of the press,* which also implies the freedom to found new publications. The constitutional limitations of this freedom are given by the provisions of Article 30 paragraphs 6 and 7 of the Constitution which, with a view to protecting certain important human, State and public values, forbids those texts which are prejudicial to the dignity, honour or privacy of persons, which infringe upon the right to one's own image, which represent defamation of the country and of the nation, which are an instigation to a war of aggression or to national, racial, class or religious hatred, which incite to discrimination, territorial separatism or public violence, and which may be classified as obscene conduct contrary to morality. Such publications shall be prohibited by law. The existence of certain juridical references for the exercise of freedom of expression also implies the juridical responsibility for the transgression of these limits, which means an abuse of right.

Similar provisions to those under Article 30 can be found in CFREU (Article 11 – Freedom of expression and information), in ECHR (Article 10 – Freedom of thought, conscience and religion) and also in ESCR (Article 29 – The right to information and consultation in collective redundancy procedures).

The *right to political association* is viewed in a similar way. Thus, Article 40 paragraph 2 of the Constitution pronounces as unconstitutional any political parties or organizations which, by their aims or activity, militate against political pluralism, the principles of a State governed by the rule of law, or against the sovereignty, integrity or independence of Romania. These restrictions originate in the historical experience of Romanian people, especially in the period of the communist one-party system. Another limitation is represented by the restriction on secret associations.

184. Religious freedom is not possible without freedom of cults. According to Article 29 paragraph 3, religious cults shall be free and organized in accordance with their own statutes. At the same time, paragraph 5 of this Article provides that religious cults shall be autonomous from the State and shall enjoy support from it,[98] including facilitation of religious assistance in the army, hospitals, prisons, homes and orphanages. The only constitutional restriction of this freedom – also deduced from the historical experience of cohabitation of several religious cults on the country's territory – is given by Article 29 paragraph 4, according to which any forms, means, acts or actions of religious enmity shall be prohibited in the relationships among the cults.[99]

Freedom of conscience, particularly religious freedom, also implies a right provided by the last paragraph of Article 29, according to which parents or legal tutors have the right to ensure, in accordance with their own convictions, the education of the minor children for whom they are responsible.

Similar provisions to those enshrined under Article 29 can be found in CFREU (Article 10 – Freedom of thought, conscience and religion) and also in ECHR (Article 9 – Freedom of thought, conscience and religion).[100]

The right of those who, according to the law, are exempted from compulsory military service because of conscientious objection (Article 42 paragraph 2 item a) has the same significance.[101] As a matter of fact, Article 42 of the Constitution (entitled 'Prohibition of forced labour') enshrines in its first paragraph a right that is asserted by negation – the right *not to be subject* to forced labour – while the second paragraph lists a number of situations that should not be considered 'forced labour'. These provisions are resonant with provisions found in CFREU (Article 5

98. In Romania, the relationship between the Church and the State is legally regulated by a complex of norms, based on the provisions of the Constitution, of which the most important one is Law No. 489/2006.

99. Irina Moroianu Zlătescu, *Religion and the Secular State in Romania* (Editura IRDO, Bucureşti, 2010), pp. 9–16.

100. *Ibid.*, 17–28.

101. Meanwhile, military service has become non-compulsory in Romania.

– Prohibition of slavery and forced labour), ECHR (Article 4 – Prohibition of slavery and forced labour) and ESCR (Article 26 – The right to dignity at work).

185. The economic, social and cultural rights and freedoms refer, by their contents, to the social, material and educational conditions of the citizens, as well as to the protection of the latter. This category includes:

> the right to education, the right to health protection, the right to work, labour social protection including interdiction of forced labour, the right to strike, the right to property, the right of inheritance, the right to a decent living standard, the right to marriage, the right to protection and assistance for children and the young, and the right to special protection of persons with disabilities.

Generally, socio-economic rights and freedoms have a complex nature in which the duty-right character prevails. Of course, it depends on the nature of the right. Thus, since it is a real right, the right to property is opposable *erga omnes,* and its features also influence the right of inheritance.

186. The right to property. The main features of the constitutional regime of property refer to several essential aspects, including: classification of property into public, with a restrictive and exceptional character, and private, which constitutes the common law; constitutional safeguard of private property and its inviolable nature; possibility of forced passing of private possessions into public property only by way of expropriation on grounds of public utility against just compensation paid in advance or by way of confiscation of goods intended for, used or resulting from a criminal or minor offence; equal protection of private property, thus putting an end to the practice of the previous regime related to unequal protection of the various types of property; extension of the constitutional safeguard of property to the State's debts as well.

The right to property, as well as the right of inheritance, is therefore accompanied by the general obligation of restraint and thus provides maximum protection for the holder.

187. The right to a decent living standard is only sanctioned by the State's obligation of means for the achievement of the policies such a living standard depends. For this reason, it is a duty-right in nature which nevertheless does not confer the effective protection of direct coercion means, by way of a lawsuit, for instance. The State is not obliged to restrain itself; on the contrary, it is obliged to do something which, however, depends on many other elements of political, social, economic, international, etc., nature. That is why such a right does not have, in a strictly juridical sense, a holder; it can only have a beneficiary. Moreover, the achievement of the right also depends on the beneficiary's participation, both as an individual and as member of a group: it depends on his active role in reaching the extent to which his right is achieved. It is a cooperation right, which means that its debt character is less precise since its achievement largely necessitates action by the beneficiary himself.

The other rights oriented towards social protection are similar. These rights, in accordance with the social nature of the State, also imply obligations of means.

They refer to the adoption of measures to support the most disadvantaged social categories, bearing in mind the high social costs of the transition towards a competing, market economy, to some measures of protection and assistance for the young, children and handicapped persons, as well as to measures to protect the public health and hygiene, to labour social protection measures including payment of unemployment aid, etc.

188. A particular case is that of *freedom of work* and *the right to strike*. Freedom of work, like property, is sanctioned by a general negative obligation, mainly referring to the interdiction of forced labour. From this point of view, it confers on the holder a direct and maximum juridical protection. Since its correlative is a resulting obligation, mere infringement of this obligation provides an effective sanction of the freedom of work.

The strike is a fundamental right consecrated by Article 43. Provisions referring to the right to strike are found in CFREU (Article 28 – Right of collective bargaining and action) and, of course, in ESCR (Article 6 – The right to bargain collectively; Article 5 – The right to organize). The right to strike and the constitutional consecration of collective labour bargaining (Article 41 paragraph 5) are illustrative of the constitutional view regarding labour social protection. Provisions related to labour and the social protection of labour (Article 41 of the Constitution) can also be found in CFREU (Article 15 – Freedom to choose an occupation and right to engage in work; Article 31 – Fair and just working conditions; Article 34 – Social security and social assistance). However, as expected, the regional instrument that devoted an ample space to the issues related to labour and its social protection is the ESCR (Article 1 – The right to work; Article 2 – The right to just conditions of work; Article 3 – The right to safe and healthy working conditions; Article 4 – The right to a fair remuneration; Article 8 – The right of employed women to protection of maternity; Article 9 – The right to vocational guidance; Article 10 – The right to vocational training; Article 27 – The right of workers with family responsibilities to equal opportunities and equal treatment; Article 28 – The right of workers' representatives to protection in the undertaking and facilities to be accorded to them).

While these aspects are fundamental, as they are the main instruments of the unions, others are also worth mentioning: weekends, paid annual leave, the normal duration of a working day, equal wages for men and women, etc.

189. Undoubtedly, the right to strike and the right to collective bargaining are generally related to the right to work. However, since they are not a purpose in themselves but a means to provide effectiveness of other rights, particularly labour protection, they can be included in the category of guarantee-rights, the last in the typology we are presenting here. However, since socio-economic and cultural rights are generally sanctioned by an obligation of means and not by one of results, the beneficiary of the right is not in a position to impose the adoption of the necessary protection measures but, depending on the adopted measures, he can be the beneficiary of an adjacent and subordinated right resulting from his constitutional right, and he can impose the observance thereof by way of disputes or by some other way.

Therefore, there are also mediated rights that provide effectiveness of the constitutional rights. This feature is most obvious with the right to marriage which, according to Article 48 of the Constitution, includes both the freedom to get married and parents' rights and duties towards their children.

At regional European level, provisions related to marriage and the family are found in CFREU (Article 9 – Right to marry and right to found a family; Article 33 – Family and professional life) and also in ECHR (Article 12 – Right to marry).

190. The right to education, provided by Article 32 of the Constitution, holds a special position; this is so because it is partly doubled by an obligation of result, that is, the compulsory general education, which necessarily is free of charge, and also by a provision regarding the autonomy of the Universities. According to the Constitution, education should be ideologically, politically and religiously neutral. Freedom of religious education is guaranteed to the denominations. In public schools, religious education is optional.

With a view to achieving pluralism in the field of education, private schools, which mostly function in the field of higher education, shall be organized according to the law.

Similar provisions to those under Article 32 related to the right to education can be found in CFREU (Article 14 – Right to education) and ECHR-P1 (Article 2 – The right to education).

The revised Constitution of 2003 introduced a couple of new rights.

Thus, Article 33 provides for *the right to access to culture*. According to paragraph 1, access to culture is guaranteed under the law. Paragraphs 2 and 3 explain what this right consists of, namely, a person's freedom to develop his spirituality and to get access to the values of national and universal culture. It also implies that the State should make sure that spiritual identity is preserved, national culture is supported, arts are stimulated, cultural legacy is protected and preserved, contemporary creativity is developed, and Romania's cultural and artistic values are promoted throughout the world.

Similar provisions to those under Article 33 can be found in CFREU (Article 13 – Freedom of the arts and sciences; Article 22 – Cultural, religious and linguistic diversity).

191. The right to a healthy environment is acknowledged in Article 35. The experience accumulated after December 1989, when various businesses developed at the cost of the quality of the environment, with adverse effects upon the entire ecosystem, doubled by an increasing worldwide concern related to the degradation of the environment as a result of human activities, was probably the main reason for the introduction of an article devoted to this issue. Unfortunately, the text is not very specific. After acknowledging the right of every person to a healthy, well-preserved and balanced environment in paragraph 1, the next two paragraphs only refer to the general obligation of the State to provide the legal framework for the exercise of this right and to the obligation of natural and legal persons to protect and improve the environment.

Provisions related to the protection of the environment can also be found in CFREU in its Article 37 – Environmental protection.

192. There are rights which, by their contents, basically have the role of providing effectiveness of the established rights and freedoms. These are the so-called guarantee-rights. In order of importance, the first one is the right to free access to justice. It is for this reason that the Constitution provides for it in the chapter dedicated to common provisions of the declaration of rights proper. The Constituent Assembly viewed free access to justice as a fundamental principle. Article 21 of the Constitution allows for the defence of any right or freedom and of any legitimate interest which is protected by the Constitution or other laws.

Correspondence of the provisions of Article 21 of the Constitution is found in CFREU (Article 47 – Right to an effective remedy and to a fair trial; Article 48 – Presumption of innocence and right of defence) and in the ECHR in its Article 6 – Right to a fair trial.

The Constitution provides that justice shall be rendered, in the name of the law, by judges who are independent and irremovable and who shall obey nothing but the law (Articles 124 and following). At the institutional level, justice is rendered by the High Court of Cassation and Justice and the other courts provided for by the law. The absolute character of this right mainly results from the provisions of paragraph 2 of Article 21, according to which no law can restrict free access to justice. It is possible to address justice for the defence of citizens' legitimate rights, freedoms and interests either by way of a direct action or by any other procedural way, including the plea of unconstitutionality.

193. The plea of unconstitutionality concerns the procedure of controlling the constitutionality of a law or ordinance. It is triggered by a court, ex officio or on request by a party who challenges the constitutional legality of the respective law or ordinance. The resolution of the plea falls, according to Article 146 paragraph (c) of the Constitution, within the exclusive competence of the Constitutional Court, as part of the *a posteriori* control upon the law. To this end, the Constitutional Court is intimated by the judge by way of demurral and the proceedings take place on the basis of the opinions of the Chambers of Parliament and Government, the report prepared and the evidence gathered by a rapporteur-judge. They are held in public session to which the parties and the Public Ministry are summoned. The decision is given by a panel consisting of three judges. The dissatisfied party can challenge the decision within ten days; the challenge also takes place in a public session and is judged by another panel of five judges. The plea of unconstitutionality is based upon the joint constitutionality control by the Constitutional Court and the ordinary court. It provides the citizens' access to the triggering and holding of the procedure and, basically, constitutes an action of public law with participation in written form of the main authorities involved in the legislative process, namely the Chambers of Parliament and the Government.

194. The contentious matters falling within the competence of the administrative courts are another procedural way having the value of constitutional safeguard of the citizens' fundamental rights and freedoms. The constitutional basis of this procedure is Article 52 of the Constitution, according to which any person aggrieved in his legitimate right by an administrative act or failure of a public authority to solve his application within the legal term is entitled to the acknowledgement of his right, annulment of the act and remedies for the damage.

195. The right to petition provided for by Article 51 of the Constitution is to be given the same meaning as guarantee rights. According to this Article, citizens have the right to apply to the public authorities by petitions formulated only in the name of the signatories.

The provisions under Article 51 of the Constitution related to the right to petition are reflected at European level in such instruments as CFREU (Article 44 – Right to petition) and ECHR (Article 13 – Right to an effective remedy).

The People's Advocate Institution, whose role is similar to that of the Ombudsman in other countries, is another constitutional safeguard of the citizens' rights and freedoms is the institution of.

As has already been shown, *the right to strike* is also to be included in the category of guaranteerights. However, unlike other guarantee rights that have a general value, according to Article 43 paragraph 1, the strike is an exclusive right of employees and it can be exercised only in the defence of their professional, economic and social interests. At the same time, paragraph 2 of Article 43 leaves to the lawmaker the possibility to establish the conditions and limits governing the exercise of this right, as well as the safeguards necessary to ensure the essential services for the society. Also, a guarantee right is the right to collective bargaining, since its purpose is to guarantee the rights of employees, including their social protection, which represents a constitutional right.

As a conclusion to the discussion on constitutional safeguards, the two most important aspects, related to the prior control of the constitutionality of laws and the rigid nature of the Constitution, should be mentioned.

The obligation of the lawmaker to ensure compliance of the law with the constitutional provisions is a direct result of the supremacy of the Constitution. It is only in complying with the Constitution that a law expresses the general will. Prior control of the law (before promulgation) allows for the checking by the Constitutional Court of the constitutional legitimacy of an adopted law, on intimation by the authorities listed in Article 146 paragraph (a) of the Constitution, namely, the President of Romania, the President of either of the two Chambers, the Government, the High Court of Cassation and Justice and at least fifty Deputies or at least twenty-five Senators. The objection of unconstitutionality may be based on any of the constitutional provisions, including those referring to the fundamental rights and freedoms, and is thus a safeguard of their supremacy within the legislative process. Therefore, in the case of prior control on the constitutionality of laws, the citizens are mere beneficiaries, the holders of the intimation right being the above-mentioned authorities. The procedure is effective in its preventive role, mainly owing to the political play of the parliamentary minorities of the opposition which, by virtue of their position, are interested in bringing the debate on the constitutional legitimacy of certain provisions adopted by the majority before the Constitutional Court.

196. An extremely important safeguard for the fundamental rights and freedoms is also the rigid nature of the Constitution. This is obvious, especially when considering the provisions of Article 152 paragraph 2, according to which – as has been shown – no revision shall be made if it results in the suppression of the citizens' fundamental rights and freedoms, or the safeguards thereof. What is meant by constitutional safeguards is not only the means of defending these rights but also the provisions of Article 152 paragraph 2 themselves. Consequently, the interdiction to suppress constitutional rights and freedoms or safeguards thereof has an absolute character at its utmost, as it also refers to the constitutional text that enshrined this interdiction. For this reason, paragraph 2 of Article 152 represents a 'petrified' constitutional provision.

§2. Minorities Issues

197. As far as the issue of minorities is concerned, in Romania, it is only applicable to persons belonging to ethnic minorities. Regarding religious faith, equality among the denominations has raised no serious problems, since it has been traditional, at least ever since the dominant position of the Orthodox cult under the Constitution of 1923, on the ground that it was the denomination of the majority of the population, was eliminated. Linguistic minorities – such as the Aromanians – only represent a problem if, at the same time, they are also an ethnic minority.

198. Romania's population, which according to the latest census of 2022 amounts to 19,053,815, is made up of a large majority of Romanians – 14,801,442, while the remainder represents more than seventeen ethnic minorities. Of these, it is only the Hungarians that represent a significant proportion, that is 1,002,151 persons – the other ethnic minorities being, in the order of their size: Gypsies (569,477), Ukrainians (45,835), Germans (22,907), Turks (20,945), Russians-Lippovans (19,394); Tartars (18,156), Serbians, Croations, Slovenians (16,868), Slovaks (10,232), Bulgarians (5,975), Greeks (2,086), Jews (2,378), Czechs (1,576), Poles (2,137), Armenians (1,213), other minorities (26,117). Of these minorities, three are spread over almost all the counties of the country: the Hungarian minority (which is a majority in two counties), the Gypsies and the Germans.

The fact that the Romanians represent the majority of the population is the outcome of the historical evolution which also resulted from the fact that numerous populations of Romanian origin (over 6 million) were included in the neighbouring States, the country being constituted of those territories where the Romanian population was compact or formed an overwhelming majority. This is true with the exception of the Republic of Moldavia, which is ethnically a second Romanian State.

199. The system for the protection of persons belonging to national minorities enshrined by the Constitution is based on the equal status of citizens. This protection provides them, on grounds of equality, access without any discrimination to all constitutional rights and freedoms of the citizens. In this respect, Article 4 paragraph 2 proclaims that Romania is the common and indivisible land of all its citizens, without any discrimination on account of race, nationality, ethnic origin, language, religion, sex, opinion, political adherence, property or social origin. Accordingly, Article 6 paragraph 1 provides that the State shall recognize and guarantee the right of persons belonging to national minorities to the preservation, development and expression of their ethnic, cultural, linguistic and religious identity. The right to identity enshrined by this Article has not the meaning of a discrimination prohibited by the Constitution; on the contrary, it allows for the establishment of a protection system to the end of achieving a real equality between the citizens of Romanian ethnic origin and those having another nationality. In this respect, paragraph 2 of Article 6 provides that the protective measures taken by the State for the preservation, development, and expression of identity of the persons belonging to national minorities shall conform to the principles of equality and non-discrimination in relation to the other Romanian citizens.

The Constitution includes several specific safeguards in terms of protection of the right to identity. These include citizens' equality before the law and public authorities (Article 16); representation ex officio in the Chamber of Deputies of organizations belonging to national minorities which, even when having not met the number of votes necessary for the election of at least one Deputy, can enjoy a certain representation (Article 62 paragraph 2); assertion of the principle of local autonomy and the principle of decentralization of public services in public administration in territorial-administrative units (Article 120). In relation to Article 120, it is worth mentioning that the respective article was added a second paragraph in the revised text of 2003, which stipulates that 'in the territorial-administrative units where citizens belonging to a national minority have a significant weight, provision shall be made for the oral and written use of that national minority's language in the relations with the local public administration authorities and the decentralized public services, under the terms stipulated by the organic law'.

Other constitutional safeguards of the right to identity refer to such aspects as: institutionalization of the popular legislative initiative; recognition of the right to use one's mother tongue in front of criminal investigation authorities (Article 23 paragraph 5) and the courts (Article 128 paragraph 2),[102] as well as the right to be educated in this language (Article 32 paragraph 3); safeguard of the right of association, political parties included, without any restrictions based on ethnic origin

102. While the corresponding article in the Constitution of 1991 (Art. 127) consisted of only two paragraphs, Art. 128 in the revised Constitution of 2003 was further developed into four paragraphs: '(1) The legal procedure shall be conducted in Romanian. (2) Romanian citizens belonging to national minorities have the right to express themselves in their mother tongue before the courts of law, under the terms of the organic law. (3) The ways for exercising the right stipulated under paragraph (2), including the use of interpreters or translations, shall be stipulated so as not to hinder the proper administration of justice and not to involve additional expenses to those interested. (4) Foreign citizens and stateless persons who do not understand or do not speak the Romanian language shall be entitled to take cognizance of all the file papers and proceedings, to speak in court and draw conclusions, by means of an interpreter; in criminal law suits, this right is ensured free of charge.'

(Article 40 paragraph 1);[103] enshrining of the freedom of religious beliefs (Article 29 paragraph 1) as well as the freedom of religious education in state-owned schools, in accordance with the requirements of each denomination (Article 32 paragraph 7); the priority of the regulations regarding human rights in case a conflict with other internal regulations occurs, etc.

There are a number of particularly important issues in relation to persons belonging to national minorities, which should be dealt with separately.

200. The first such important issue is *education*. According to Article 32 paragraph 3 of the Constitution, the right of persons belonging to national minorities to learn their mother tongue and their right to be educated in this language are guaranteed. To this end, as provided by the general regulations regarding the organization of education, the localities with populations from among the national minorities have kindergartens, primary and secondary schools, high schools, regular schools, classes, groups or sections where the teaching language is the respective mother tongue, depending on the requests and the proportion of the population belonging to minorities in the respective area. At the level of higher education, there are specific ways to further minority languages (in some of the disciplines, sections, groups and institutions).

201. As far as *freedom of religion* is concerned, the different cults functioning in Romania[104] are given the possibility to use their mother tongue in all their specific activities and to offer moral-religious education in schools. The State, on the basis of the support it is obliged to provide according to the Constitution, covers part of the wages of the clergy and the full wages of the teaching staff in theology schools.[105] At the same time, the State provides funds for the building and repairing of churches.

As a rule, national minorities and denominations do not overlap, meaning that national minorities do not belong to one denomination only. Thus, most persons of Hungarian ethnic origin belong to the Reformed and Unitarian denomination; however, some of them belong to the Roman-Catholic, the Evangelic Synod-Presbyterian, the Baptist, the Adventist of the Seventh Day, the Pentecostal and the Christian after the Gospel denominations. Nevertheless, there also are minorities belonging to a single denomination, such as the Armenians who exclusively belong to the Armenian Church, the Lippovans who belong to the Christian Church of Old

103. Provisions dealing with the right of association can also be found in CFREU (Art. 12 – Freedom of assembly and of association) and also in ECHR (Art. 11 – Freedom of assembly and association).
104. These cults are (descending order as to the number of believers): Roman-Catholic Church, Greek-Catholic Church, Reformed Church, Evangelic Catholic Church, Lutheran Church, Unitarian Church, Armenian Church, Christian Church of Old Rite, Union of Christian Baptist Churches, Pentecostal Union, Adventist Christian Church, Gospel Church, Romanian Evangelic Church, Muslim Cult, Mosaic Cult.
105. According to the most recent regulations regarding education (Law 198/2023 regarding the pre-university education and 199/2023 regarding university education, updated and modified by Law No. 6/9.1.2026, respectively Law No. 17/15.1.2026), aside from public/state religious education, private confesional institutions were financially endorsed, in order to offer free access to religious education.

Rite, the Jews who observe Mosaic Judaism, the Turks and Tartars who are Muslim, the Croatians who are all Catholic, etc.

202. Cultural Life. The most representative minorities have, as far as theatre and folklore are concerned, a stable institutional framework (seven dramatic theatres, three puppet theatres, a lyrical theatre and three artistic ensembles belonging to the Hungarian minority, in addition to the amateur movement; two dramatic theatres, one puppet theatre and a rich amateur movement as far as the German minority is concerned; a Jewish theatre in Yiddish – the only one in Europe – and amateur ensembles, etc.). Generally, however, cultural ensembles – theatres, choirs, folk ensembles – are amateur ones.

In terms of the written and the audio-visual press, there are nineteen titles of magazines and periodicals edited in the languages of national minorities with subsidies from the State. On the national stations of radio and television, there are two broadcasts in Hungarian, two in German and one for the other minorities, in addition to the more diverse broadcasts of the territorial stations.

There are also publishing houses specialized in the languages of national minorities, particularly the Hungarian and the German, as well as museums, memorial houses and cultural and religious monuments specific to the culture of national minorities.

203. As regards *participation in the political life* of the country, on the basis of the right of association, persons belonging to national minorities have set up their own organizations. The Magyar Democratic Union of Romania (Uniunea Democratică a Maghiarilor din Romania, 'UDMR') was set up on 22 December 1989, the date of the revolution. According to Article 62 paragraph 2 of the Constitution and the corresponding provisions of Article 9 of Law No. 35/2008,[106] provided that they have a certain representativeness – at least 10% of the average number of votes per country necessary for the election of one Deputy – these organizations have the right to one Deputy seat by designation, unless they were successful in the elections. Thus, with the exception of the UDMR, which has a significant representation resulting from the elections both in the Chamber of Deputies and in the Senate – entitling it to have a Parliament Group in each Chamber – the other minorities are represented by one Deputy each, the organizations of these minorities forming a specific Parliament Group in the Chamber of Deputies.

At local level, the bodies of local autonomy – Mayors and Local Councils – are constituted on an electoral basis. As a result, in many localities, depending on the proportion of persons belonging to national minorities, these authorities are made up of citizens belonging to national minority groups. This feature is more conspicuous where such groups are the majority. Most Mayors, Deputy Mayors and Councillors from among persons belonging to national minorities are Hungarians and Germans.

106. Law 35/2008 on electing the Chamber of Deputies and the Senate amended and supplemented: Law No. 67/2004 on electing the authorities of the local public administration, Law No. 215/2001 on the local public administration, and Law No. 393/2004 on the status of the local elected, with the subsequent amendments and supplementations.

At central level, within the framework of the central administration, the Council for National Minorities functions in subordination to the Government. The Council is an advisory body of the Government, coordinated by the Secretary General thereof. It is made up of representatives of the organizations belonging to national minorities and of the main Ministries and central bodies, and has the task to give advisory opinions on or to initiate normative acts concerning the issues of national minorities, to debate some local problems and take the necessary measures for their resolution, to establish permanent contacts with the organizations of minorities and to solve the problems it is addressed with by the respective organizations, etc.

204. Another important issue to be discussed in relation to the protection of the identity of national minorities is *justice*. Article 128 of the Constitution provides that citizens belonging to national minorities, as well as persons who cannot speak Romanian, have the right to take cognizance of all acts and files of the case and to speak before the court and formulate conclusions through an interpreter. In criminal trials, this right shall be ensured free of charge. Thus, by the institutionalization of the right to have an interpreter, free access to justice for persons belonging to national minorities is ensured. The right to an interpreter thus also has the role of a guarantee right to free access to justice for the benefit of persons belonging to national minorities. The same meaning is to be given to Article 23 paragraph 5 of the Constitution, stating that any person detained or arrested shall be promptly informed, in a language he understands, of the grounds for his detention or arrest, and notified of the charges against him.

Similar provisions to those included under Article 22 can be found in CFREU (Article 6 – Right to liberty and security), ECHR (Article 5 – Right to liberty and security) and also in ESCR (Article 12 – The right to social security).

205. Everything that has been said so far illustrates that the rights of persons belonging to national minorities are part of the fundamental human rights and freedoms. That is why an essential role in the definition of the constitutional and legal character of these rights is held by the principle of equality of all citizens. On the basis of this principle, the right to identity of the persons belonging to national minorities represents a specific principle which, in respect of these persons, ensures either the application in a certain way of the constitutional rights and freedoms generally recognized for citizens, or certain particular rights and safeguards. Substantially, the status of persons belonging to national minorities concerns their right to have their own cultural-spiritual life and to have unlimited access to the country's social, political and economic life and thereby benefit from the opportunities offered by the development of the Romanian society.

§3. Judicial Control of Administrative Action

206. The European constitutional systems, as was shown, are based on the principle of the separation of powers. Separation of powers, in its turn, is based on what the doctrine calls the 'checks and balances' system – a formula consisting of a mechanism of mutual control among the three powers meant to maintain a functional balance among them.

In Romania, the Constitution of 1923 imparted the administrative dispute matters to the judiciary under a special law that was in effect up to the installation of the totalitarian regime.

It is not difficult to guess that during dictatorial regimes, administrative acts cannot be challenged before a court of justice. Romania was no exception till the year 1967. In that year, a law on the judicial control of the acts of the State administration was adopted, but it was insufficient, on the one hand, because of the narrow and unessential area of administrative acts that could be challenged, and on the other hand, because of the mistrust of the population towards the competent courts of law, as the latter tended to reject such challenges.

The Constitution proclaims in its Article 52(1) that:

> Any person aggrieved in his/her legitimate rights or interests by a public authority, by means of an administrative act or by the failure of a public authority to solve his/her application within the lawful time limit, is entitled to the acknowledgement of his claimed right or legitimate interest, the annulment of the act and reparation for the damage.

Paragraph 2 of the cited Article provides that the conditions for and limits on the exercise of this right shall be regulated by an organic law. In application of this constitutional provision, Law No. 554 of 2 December 2004 on administrative disputes was adopted.[107]

207. According to the law, any person who considers one of his rights or legitimate interests to have been encroached upon by a public authority under an administrative act or by failure to solve his application within the legal time limit, may address the competent court of administrative disputes for annulment of the act, recognition of the claimed right or legitimate interest and redress for the damage that was caused to him. The legitimate interest may be both private and public (Article 1 paragraph 1 of Law No. 554/2004).

According to paragraph 2 of the same Article, the court of administrative disputes can also be intimated by a person aggrieved in his right or legitimate interest by an individualized administrative act, addressed to another subject of law.

If the petitioner does not receive an answer within thirty days since the respective application was registered, the respective authority is considered to have refused to solve the petitioner's application, unless the law provides for another term. Administrative-jurisdictional acts may, in principle, be challenged by way of

107. The initial text has been amended and supplemented by: Emergency Ordinance No. 190/2005; Decision No. 189/2006; Decision No. 647/2006; Decision No. 65/2007; Decisions No. 660/2007; Rectification No. 797/2007; Law No. 97/2008; Law No. 100/2008; Law No. 202/2010; Decision No. 1069/2010, and others, the latest by Law No. 107/2022.

appeal, after the administrative-jurisdictional ways have been exhausted, within fifteen days since notification before the administrative disputes section of the High Court of Cassation and Justice, which shall pronounce a final decision.

According to the law, applications shall be solved under special procedure. It starts with the requirement that the application should first be addressed to the issuing authority, which is bound to respond to the petition within thirty days. The person who is dissatisfied with the received answer, or whose petition was not answered, may address the court of law.

208. The competence to rule on administrative disputes falls upon the county tribunal or the tribunal of the municipality of Bucharest, in whose jurisdiction the petitioner's domicile is.

Under a speedy procedure, the tribunal rules on the petitions in a two-judge panel. It may annul, totally or partially, the administrative act, or oblige the administrative authority to issue an administrative act, an authorization, a certificate, or any other document. The tribunal also has the competence to pronounce a judgment regarding the legality of the administrative acts or operations that are the basis of the issue of the contested act, and it may also pronounce a decision regarding the material and moral redress that shall be granted to the victim. According to the law, the proceedings before the tribunal may also be instituted, under certain circumstances, against a public servant.

The tribunal's decision may be challenged by way of appeal. The appeal decision may be challenged by way of recourse before the High Court of Cassation and Justice within fifteen days of notification.

In both cases (appeal or recourse), execution of the act is suspended.

The appeal procedure is a speedy one. In case the appeal is admitted, the court annuls the judgment, while re-judging the disputed matter on the merits.

The High Court of Cassation and Justice, the courts of appeal and the tribunals have special sections for administrative disputes.

§4. The Status of Aliens

209. The Constitution does include provisions related to the status of aliens. The legislation adopted to detail the constitutional provisions related to aliens includes Emergency Ordinance No. 194 of 12 December 2002[108] on the status of aliens in Romania. All these normative acts refer, among other things, to the rights and the duties of aliens in Romania.

108. This ordinance abolished Law No. 123/2001 on the status of aliens in Romania. Since 2002, Emergency Ordinance No. 194 has been amended and supplemented several times, by: Law No. 357/2003, Law No. 309/2004, Law No. 482/2004, Emergency Ordinance 113/2005, Law No. 306/2005, Law No. 56/2007, Emergency Ordinance 55/2007, Law No. 347/2007, and Emergency Ordinance No. 12/2010. The latest amendments and supplementations are very recent and were introduced by Law No. 157/2011, Government Ordinance 25/26.8.2014, Government Ordinance

The rights include:

1. Aliens who are legally residing in Romania shall enjoy the general protection of persons and fortunes, guaranteed by the Constitution and other law, as well as the rights laid down in the international treaties where Romania is a party.
2. Aliens who reside legally in Romania may freely travel and establish their residence or, as the case may be, their home anywhere on the territory of Romania.
3. Aliens having their residence or domicile in Romania shall enjoy social protection from the Romanian State on equal terms with Romanian citizens.
4. Aliens enrolled in educational units of all ranks shall enjoy unrestricted access to all school and instruction activities within the Romanian society, etc.

Aliens' obligations include:

1. Throughout their stay in Romania, aliens shall observe the Romanian legislation.
2. Aliens may not organize on the territory of Romania political parties and they may not become members of existing political parties either, may not hold public positions and dignities; also, they may not initiate, organize or participate in demonstrations or meetings that are violating public order or national security.
3. Aliens may not finance political parties, organizations, groups or demonstrations or meetings.
4. While on the territory of Romania, aliens shall be bound to observe the purpose for which they were granted the right to enter Romania, etc.

Other legal provisions refer to immigration, the right to asylum, and regulating the conditions under which asylum may be granted.

210. The relatively large number of normative acts in the field can be explained, on the one hand, on the fact that Romania had to harmonize its legislation in the field of aliens with that of the EU prior to become a Member State of the EU and, on the other hand, on the fact that once a member country of the EU, the Romanian legislation had to reflect this new reality, also by making a distinction between foreigners who were citizens of another EU country and those who were citizens of a non-EU country. At the same time, in terms of immigration, from a transit country, Romania has gradually become a target country.

Now coming back to the Constitution, the relevant constitutional text is to be found in several articles. Thus, Article 18 of the Constitution provides that aliens and stateless persons living in Romania shall enjoy general protection of person and

---

25/24.8.2014, Law No. 247/2018, GEO 14/2021, Law No. 22/2022 on amending and supplementing some normative acts regarding the status of aliens in Romania. There were also supplementations given the 2024-2025 legislation, which distinguishes between EU/Swiss/European Economic Area citizens and citizens from non-EU countries.

assets, as guaranteed by the Constitution and other laws. As far as the right to asylum is concerned, it is provided in paragraph 2 of the same Article that it shall be granted and withdrawn under the provisions of the law, in compliance with the international treaties and covenants Romania is a party to.

These provisions of principle are corroborated by other constitutional texts. Thus, according to Article 57, Romanian citizens, aliens and stateless persons shall exercise their constitutional rights and freedoms in good faith, without any infringement of the rights and liberties of others.

Another text worth mentioning in this context is that of Article 44 paragraph 2 of the Fundamental Act. The text provides that private property shall be equally guaranteed and protected by the law, irrespective of its owner. Foreign citizens and stateless persons shall only acquire the right to private property of land under the terms resulting from Romania's accession to the EU and other international treaties Romania is a party to, on a mutual basis, under the terms stipulated by an organic law, as well as a result of lawful inheritance. As far as the regional human rights instruments are concerned, the right to property is also enshrined under CFREU (Article 17 – Right to property) and also under the ECHR-P1 (Article 1 – Protection of property).

§5. Conclusion of or Adherence to International Treaties

211. In the field of foreign policy, it is not only to periods of serious crisis, such as armed conflicts, that the President's powers refer to, but also to normal relations of cooperation and peaceful collaboration between States. In this respect, the President of Romania, in his capacity as Head of State, signs international treaties in the name of Romania. The legitimacy of these treaties is, constitutionally, threefold. They are negotiated by the Government, which implies approval of the negotiated treaty by the Government members before it is submitted to the President for signature. They are ratified through a law by Parliament, which also implies the control on the constitutionality of the ratification law by the Constitutional Court if it is intimated to this end. Finally, they are submitted to the President for ratification of the treaty by the President within sixty days from their signing. Thus, preeminence of the legislature is provided in this field as well, taking into account the institutionalization, through the Constitution, of the 'self-execution' of international conventions.

Therefore, the President's powers are limited to the international conventions concluded in the name of Romania. By way of consequence, other international commitments, concluded by the Government and other public authorities, shall be established according to the powers they have.

§6. Foreign Policy

212. In terms of foreign policy, the President's powers refer to the organization of the country's diplomatic relations. The President, on proposal by the Government, accredits and recalls Romania's diplomatic envoys and approves the setting up, closing down or change in rank of diplomatic missions. Regarding the diplomatic envoys of other States, they are accredited before the President of Romania.

However, it is the Government that is responsible for the management of the country's foreign policy. It is the reason why the decrees by which the President exercises his powers in this field must be countersigned by the Prime Minister.

And of course, in consonance with the principle of separation of powers, Parliament has an important role in the field of foreign policy, not only due to its constitutional pre-eminence in the framework of the political regime but also as a result of the development of parliamentary diplomacy to the end of gradually integrating the country into the European cooperation structures.

§7. Euro-Atlantic Integration

213. It was pointed out at the beginning of this discussion on the Constitution of Romania that the need for revising a Constitution in general may arise earlier than the doctrine would be willing to accept, when the political, economic, and social circumstances impose such a revision. It was also pointed out that a similar situation, characterized by the historic imperatives of Romania's integration into NATO and the EU, as well as the peculiarities of the transition period, was faced by Romania in the year 2004.

Well, Romania's Euro-Atlantic integration, which in 2004 started to turn from a quasi-unanimous desideratum of the nation into a palpable reality, was one of the very reasons why the Constitution of 1991 had to be revised, such as to reflect the new realities.

From a juridical point of view, adherence of a state to the EU presupposes ratification of several international treaties, called the 'EU Constitutive Treaties' by the constitutional text. Romania's Constitution of 1991 included general provisions referring to the ratification of international treaties (Article 11) and special provisions referring only to the ratification of international treaties in the field of human rights (Article 20). However, it lacked general provisions referring to the transfer of certain State powers under the competence of international organizations or to the exercise of competencies that are specifically belonging to a State in common with other States, as is the case with other European fundamental laws. The normative solution preferred by the Romanian Constitution makers was that of specific legal norms for each type of such transfer of powers or exercise of competencies in common with other States. These were grouped in a Title solely devoted to these issues. Thus, Title VI of the revised Constitution of 2003 is 'Euro-Atlantic Integration' and includes two articles. Article 148 is devoted to the integration into the EU, while Article 149 deals with accession to the North Atlantic Treaty. In order to mark the importance the Romanian State attaches to Romania's adherence to the EU, the constitutional norms provided for particular procedures for the ratification of the EU Constitutive Treaties, which derogate from the general rules established in Articles 11 and 20 of the Constitution. Paragraph 1 of Article 148 provides that:

> Romania's accession to the constituent treaties of the European Union, with a view to transferring certain powers to community institutions, as well as to

> exercising in common with the other Member States the abilities stipulated in such treaties, shall be carried out by means of a law adopted in the joint sitting of the Chamber of Deputies and the Senate, with a majority of two-thirds of the number of deputies and senators.

Therefore, the Treaty on Romania's accession to the EU shall be ratified under a law which, owing to its sui generis procedure, could not be assigned to any of the three categories of laws mentioned by Article 73 (constitutional, organic and ordinary laws).

The ratification act under which Romania adhered to the EU is not a constitutional law because neither from a structural nor from a formal point of view does it fall into this category of laws. It comes out that, at domestic level, the legal act under which Romania adheres to the EU has less legal force than the Constitution and the constitutional laws, but higher legal force than organic and ordinary laws. The adherence act is essentially (by its normative content) a law for the ratification of an international treaty, obeying the procedural rules that are characteristic of this field and the rules specified under Article 11.

The second paragraph of Article 148 deals with the delicate subject of the relationship between the community regulations and the domestic ones. The provision of paragraph 2 only consecrates the precedence of the community regulations over the domestic law, with no reference to its direct and immediate applicability.

According to Article 148, paragraph 4, corroborated with Article 80, paragraph 1, and Article 91, the Parliament, the President, the Government, and the Judicial Authority are to guarantee the 'obligations resulting from the act of accession'. While exercising his constitutional powers, the President takes part in the European Council, as the public authority that has the competency to assume obligations in the name of the Romanian State. He can expressly delegate the participation to the European Council to the Prime Minister.[109]

214. The revised Constitution of 2003 provided for certain institutional guarantees for fulfilment of the obligations coming from the status of an EU member country. Basically, these obligations refer to effective participation, to the gradual strengthening of European integration, as well as the obligations resulting from the entire European legal order.

The final paragraph 5 of Article 148 enshrines constitutionally a set of rules that are needed for a good functioning of the State authorities in the framework of participation in the EU. Thus, according to paragraph 5, the Government shall send to the two Chambers of the Parliament the draft mandatory acts before they are submitted to the EU institutions for approval. This procedure allows for Parliament's point of view to be expressed, while also taking into account the precedence of the community rules and the need to harmonize the domestic legislation with the former.

---

109. *See* the Decision of the Constitutional Court of Romania No. 683/27.6.2012, published in the Monitorul Oficial, Part I, No. 479/12.7.2012.

215. As far as Romania's accession to the North Atlantic Treaty is concerned, according to Article 149 of the Constitution, it shall take place by means of a law adopted in the joint sitting of the Chamber of Deputies and the Senate, with a majority of two-thirds of the number of deputies and senators.

The North Atlantic Treaty is a classical international organization of intergovernmental cooperation, therefore different from the EU. The North-Atlantic Treaty resulted from the free participation of the Member States and is meant at present to provide the collective defence of the Member States.

Accession to the North-Atlantic Treaty is fundamentally different from adherence to the EU, by the nature and the specificity of this particular international organization and also by the different objectives pursued by the Romanian State in the two situations. Nevertheless, the Constitution makers provided for the same type of particular adherence procedure as in the case of the EU, namely, adoption of a sui generis law for the ratification of an international treaty: adoption of the law has to be done in the joint sitting of the Chamber of Deputies and the Senate, with a majority of two-thirds of the number of deputies and senators. Even though the procedure is the same, Romania's participation in the North-Atlantic Treaty corresponds to a different type of priority of the State policy, that is, to ensure the country's security and increase its defence capacity.

§8. The Financial System

216. Before concluding this presentation of Romania's Constitution, there are a few more topics to briefly deal with.

One group of such issues refers to the budget, taxes, duties and other contributions, in other words, the financial system. All these issues are regulated by Title IV of the Constitution – Economy and public finance.

According to Article 139 paragraph 1 of the Constitution, taxes and any other revenues of the State budget and the State social security budget shall be established only by law. As regards local taxes and duties, these shall be established by the local or county councils, within the limits and under the terms of the law (Article 139 paragraph 2). According to this system, the State's revenues, both central and local, shall be established only by the public authorities directly elected by universal suffrage, that is, Parliament and Local Councils, respectively. In the hierarchy of the sources of law, the law has a pre-eminent nature in the establishment of these revenues which, at the central level, shall be approved through a legislative act having the force of law, and at the local level, shall be approved through an administrative act – the decision by the Local Council under the principle of local autonomy but only within the limits and under the terms of the law. The hierarchy of the sources of law corresponds to Parliament's competence to pass the State budget and the State social security budget, as well as that of the Local Councils to approve the local budgets.

217. The National Public Budget, as a whole, is formed by the three above-mentioned budgets. This is a constitutional concept contained in Article 138 of the

Constitution, governed by certain principles common to the three categories of budgets and by some special rules applicable to the central and local budgets. The common rules refer to the annuity principle, according to which all budgets are annual and the exercise thereof is checked at the end of the budgetary year, and the principle that the budgets shall be approved by the public authorities directly elected through universal suffrage, that is, Parliament and the Local Councils respectively. Accordingly, central budgets are approved through a law, while the local ones are approved through a decision by the Local Council – an administrative act subordinated to the law – under the conditions stipulated by the law on local autonomy. The only derogation from the annuity principle is that, if the budget has not been approved at the end of the year, the budget of the expired year is prorogued de jure until the new budget is approved. In such a case, therefore, the law adopting the expired budget is extended.

218. Central budgets are elaborated by the Government. Thus, it is the latter that holds monopoly on the legislative initiative. At the same time, since the budgets are approved through a law, they shall be subject to the control of the constitutionality of the approval law by the Constitutional Court. On the other hand, at local level, it is the Mayor who has the initiative for the elaboration of the budget, while the approval decisions may only be attacked by way of administrative disputes.

It is worth mentioning that a basic rule in the elaboration and approval of the budget is that no budgetary expenditure may be approved without having established the financing source. For this reason, Article 111 paragraph 1 of the Constitution provides that if a legislative initiative involves amendments of the budget provisions, it is compulsory that Parliament request the Government the necessary information for the establishment of the financing source.

219. An important role in the control of the budgetary exercise is held by the *Court of Audit*. The latter annually reports on the accounts of the National Public Budget administration in the expired budgetary year, including the cases of mismanagement it has found.

The constitutional provisions devoted to the Court of Audit were amended and supplemented by the revised Constitution of 2003. Thus, while according to the text of 1991 the Court of Audit had jurisdictional powers, the revised text of 2003 removed the Court's jurisdictional powers. Article 140 paragraph 1 of the Constitution of 2003 provides that, under the terms of the organic law, the disputes resulting from the activity of the Court of Audit shall be solved by specialized courts of law.

According to Article 140 of the Constitution and the provisions of its own law of organization and functioning, Law No. 94/1992, modified and updated, in principle, the Court of Audit shall exercise control on the formation, administration and use of the financing sources of the State and the public sector. The members of the Court shall be appointed by Parliament. They shall be independent, irremovable and subject to the incompatibilities the law provides for judges. By its constitutional and legal status, the Court of Audit is the specialized body through which Parliament exercises its control function regarding the field of financial discipline in the formation, administration and use of public resources, whether budgetary or extra-budgetary (special funds, approved under the law). Under the law, the Court also exercises jurisdictional powers for constituting the writs of execution in case its control bodies find the existence of damages.

§9. War and National Defence

220. According to Article 80 of the Constitution, in his capacity as Head of State, the President of Romania is responsible for the country's defence and for its unity and territorial integrity. Because of this responsibility, the President is the Commander-in-Chief of the country's armed forces, a constitutional concept including, besides the army proper, the other militarized structures of the State as well, such as the police, the frontier-guard troops, the intelligence services, etc. This capacity of the Head of State is traditional in Romania. It goes back to the period preceding the formation of the modern State, as is in fact also the case in other countries. It is because of this responsibility that the Head of State also presides over the Supreme Council of National Defence.

According to Article 92 paragraph 2 of the Constitution, the President of Romania, in his capacity as Commander-in-Chief of the Armed Forces, may declare, with prior approval of Parliament, partial or general mobilization of the armed forces. This competence shall be corroborated with Parliament's power, provided for under Article 65 letter (c), stipulating that the two Chambers united in joint session can declare general or partial mobilization. In exceptional cases, such as an imminent aggression, the decision by the President may be subsequently submitted for approval to Parliament, within five days from the adoption thereof.

Prior to making such a decision, the President must submit it for debate to the Supreme Council of National Defence. For this reason, the President's decision is not the expression of a discretionary power, all the more so since the President's decree regarding the declaration of mobilization must be countersigned by the Prime Minister and in all cases, the measure thus established shall be submitted for approval to Parliament. As a rule, such approval is given beforehand and the President therefore takes action exclusively as an executive authority. Even if, under exceptional circumstances, the President is bound to take such a measure at once, it is afterwards submitted for ratification to Parliament so that, in all cases, it is the national representatives who eventually make the decision.

221. Article 92 paragraph 3 of the Constitution provides that in case an armed aggression against the country is triggered, the President of Romania shall take measures to repel the aggression and he shall promptly bring them to the cognizance of Parliament through a message. If Parliament is not in session, it shall be convened de jure within twenty-four hours from the outbreak of the aggression. This is the consequence of the fact that, according to Article 65 letters (d) and (e) of the Constitution, it is only the two Chambers sitting in joint session that may declare a state of war or suspend or terminate armed hostilities. For this reason, even though the President, facing the emergency represented by an armed aggression, is entitled to take the necessary measures to repel it, these measures cannot have the meaning of a declaration of the state of war which, in the juridical sense of the word, is the exclusive power of Parliament in its capacity as the supreme representative body of the people, as provided under Article 61 paragraph 1 of the Constitution.

As far as peace is concerned, since it is achieved through an international treaty subject to ratification by Parliament, it is only the latter that is competent to decide. This again corresponds to its constitutional pre-eminence over the executive authority.

§10. Emergency Powers

222. Here, the revised Constitution of 2003 maintained the text of 1991. The regime of the state of siege and emergency shall be approved under an organic law, as provided under Article 73 paragraph 3, letter (e) of the Constitution. So far, such a law has not been adopted yet. The Constitution only regulates the conditions for instituting the state of siege or emergency. Thus, Article 93 of the Constitution provides that the President of Romania shall, according to the law, institute the state of siege or emergency in the whole or part of the country, and shall request Parliament's approval of the measure within five days from adoption thereof. If Parliament is not in session, it shall be convened de jure within forty-eight hours from the institution of the state of siege or emergency, and shall function throughout this State. The latter rule is a constitutional guarantee against excesses or abuses by the authorities in relation to the events that justified the proclamation of the state of siege or emergency. However, the most important constitutional guarantee related to the institution of the state of siege or emergency is given by the fact that the President's decision is subject to Parliament's approval, so that, ultimately, the very institution of the State, and not only its regime, is the expression of the legislature's will. It is true that the President has the monopoly on initiative. However, the measure may be irrevocably adopted only through the harmonized will of the two representative public authorities through which – since they are directly elected – the people directly exercise, in the spirit of Article 2 of the Constitution, national sovereignty: Parliament and the President of Romania.

§11. Constitutional Status of the Army

223. It is defined under Article 118 paragraph 1 as follows: 'The army shall be exclusively subordinated to the will of the people, to guarantee the sovereignty, independence and unity of the State, the country's territorial integrity, and constitutional democracy.' It appears from this provision that the army is not only a major component of public administration but also that no representative body may request the army to carry out other actions than those corresponding to its status, that is, representing guarantees for the sovereignty, independence and unity of the State and for the defence of democracy. The army's status is, *mutatis mutandis,* applicable to the other components of the armed forces as well, that is, all the military structures of the State, such as the police, the frontier-guard troops, the intelligence services, etc.

The monopoly on the use of armed force is held by the State. As a consequence of this principle, the Constitution prohibits the organization of military or paramilitary activities outside the framework of a State authority, and provides that foreign troops may enter or cross the country's territory only as provided by the law.

From the point of view of institutions, the Constitution establishes two rules of principle: that the President of Romania is the Commander-in-Chief of the Armed Forces; and that the Supreme Council of National Defence, whose president is the Head of State, uniquely organizes and coordinates all activities related to the country's defence and national security.

In its Article 119, the Constitution provides that the Supreme Council of National Defence shall unitarily organize and coordinate the activities concerning the country's defence and security, its participation in international security keeping, and in collective defence in military alliance systems, as well as in peace-keeping or restoring missions.

224. According to Law No. 346/2006 on the organization and functioning of the Ministry of National Defence and Law No. 415/2002, on the organization and functioning of the Supreme Council of National Defence, with the subsequent amendments, the Council includes the presidents of the legislative bodies, the Prime Minister, Ministers and other dignitaries holding offices related to the country's defence and national security. The Council submits reports to the two Chambers of Parliament sitting in joint session, thereby being responsible to Parliament for the accomplishment of its mission. By way of its constitutional status and its structure, the Supreme Council of National Defence is a public administration authority, autonomous in relation to the Government, presided by the President of Romania and subject to parliamentary control.

225. The country's defence is a national imperative, so it is related not only to the State's specialized structures but also to the entire people. For this reason, according to Article 55 of the Constitution, citizens have the right and duty to defend Romania. At the same time, paragraph 2 under Article 55 provides that the terms for doing the military service shall be set up in an organic law. According to Law No. 395 of 16 December 2005 on suspending the compulsory military service at times of peace and transition to a voluntary military service system, the compulsory military service was eliminated. It is important to point out that the compulsory military service was not eliminated altogether, but only suspended for as long as there is peace. It means that in case the country is the target of a military aggression, the compulsory military service may be reinstated. This is the reason why paragraph 3 of Article 55, according to which citizens may be conscripted from the age of 20 and up to the age of 35, except for volunteers, under the terms of the applicable organic law, is still meaningful. For the same reason, Article 118 paragraph 2 of the Constitution, according to which the structure of the national defence system, the organization of the Army, the preparation of the population, economy and territory for the defence, as well as the status of the military shall be regulated by an organic law, is also meaningful.

§12. THE CHURCH-STATE RELATIONSHIP

226. One last aspect to be dealt with at the end of this presentation is the *constitutional relationship between the Church and the State*. The relationship between the Church and the State is based on the principle of freedom of conscience.[110] According to Article 29 of the Constitution, freedom of thought, opinion, and religious beliefs may not be restricted in any form whatsoever. By way of consequence, in terms of religious freedom, according to the same Article, no one may be compelled to embrace an opinion or religion contrary to his own convictions. Accordingly, freedom of expression of any thoughts, opinions, or beliefs whatsoever, through the public media, is inviolable. It is these principles that are at the basis of Article 29 paragraph 3, according to which all religions shall be free and organized in accordance with their own statutes, under the terms laid down by the law.

It should be emphasized that, in line with the principle according to which freedom of conscience should be manifested in a spirit of tolerance and mutual respect, the Constitution prohibits, in the relationships between the religious groups, any forms, means, acts or actions of religious enmity.

The relationship between the State and the religious groups, regulated by Law No. 489/2006,[111] amended and supplemented, is characterized by autonomy, while the religious groups shall be supported by the State. Such support shall nevertheless guarantee freedom of conscience by the way religious assistance in the army, in hospitals, prisons, homes and orphanages is provided. At the same time, it includes a measure of certain financial support, like that given for building or restoring some houses of worship.

Integration under the normal circumstances created after the downfall of the Iron Curtain, Romania's joining various international structures, and its integration in the structures of the EU, made the Romanian authorities accept or consider certain evaluations, advice or recommendations on various issues.

Romania signed a large number of international documents and regulations, universal and regional, and the observance of the commitments it assumed is an essential prerequisite for Romania's present development and its integration (since 2007) in the structures of the EU. Enjoying all due attention, human rights issues include, as one important chapter, the observance of the religious and confessional freedom of conscience, belief and expression.[112]

110. Victor Dan Zlătescu. *Concepts religieux et les droits de l'homme* in *Les droits de l'homme. Dimension spirituelle et action civique* (Editura IRDO & AIF, Bucureşti, 2000), pp. 4 and the following.
111. Published in the Monitorul Oficial, Part I, No. 11/8.1.2007.
112. Moroianu Zlătescu, *Human Rights: A Dynamic and Evolving Process*, *supra*, 364–365.

Selected Bibliography

Alexandru, Ioan, *100 de ani in evoluţia dreptului administrativ din România*, in *Evolutia dreptului si a societăţii româneşti în context internaţional 1918–2018*, Bucureşti: Editura Universitară, Editura Universul Academic, 2019.

Bălan, Marius, *Drept constituţional şi instituţii politice, vol.1, Teoria Generală a statului şi a constituţiei. Constituţia română în context contemporan*, Bucureşti, Ed. Hamangiu, 2015.

Ceterchi, Ioan (coord), *Istoria dreptului românesc*, vol.2, partea I, Bucureşti, Editura Academiei, 1984.

Constantinescu, Mihai, et al., *Constituţia României revizuită. Comentarii şi explicaţii,* Bucureşti: Editura All Beck, 2004.

Dănişor, Dan Claudiu, *Putere şi autoritate constituantă în România revoluţionară*, în Pandectele Române, nr.1/2018.

Deleanu, Ion, *Instituţii şi proceduri constituţionale: în dreptul român şi în dreptul comparat,* Bucureşti: Editura C.H. Beck, 2006.

Dorneanu, Valer, *Consiliul Legislativ la 25 de ani de la reînfiinţare: dovadă vie şi elocventă a utilităţii şi importanţei sale*, in *Buletin de Informare Legislativă* nr. 2, Bucureşti: Editura Monitorul Oficial, 2021, p. 17.

Drăganu, Tudor, *Drept constituţional şi instituţii politice. Tratat elementar,* Bucureşti: Editura Lumina Lex, 2000.

Enache, Marian and Deaconu, Ştefan, *Drepturile şi libertăţile fundamentale în jurisprudenţa Curţii Constituţionale*, vols I, II, III, Bucureşti: Editura C.H. Beck, 2019.

Gionea, Vasile, et al., *Partidele politice,* Bucureşti: Editura Regia Autonomă 'Monitorul Oficial', 1993.

Iancu, Gheorghe, *Drept constituţional şi instituţii politice. Tratat,* Bucureşti: Editura C.H. Beck, 2010.

Ionescu, Cristian, *Instituţii politice şi drept constituţional*, Bucureşti: Editura Juridică, 2006.

Ionescu, Cristian, *Tratat de drept constituţional contemporan,* ed. 3, Bucureşti: Editura C.H. Beck, 2019.

Ionescu, Dionisie, Ţuţui, Gheorghe and Matei, Gheorghe, *Dezvoltarea constituțională a statului român*, Bucureşti: Editura Ştiinţifică, 1957.

Iorgovan, Antonie, *Tratat de drept administrativ,* vol. I, ed. a 4-a, Bucureşti: Editura All Beck, 2005.

Lapedatu, Alexandru, *Ion Câmpineanu (1798–1863)*, Bucureşti: Editura Cartea Românească, 1937.

Selected Bibliography

Moroianu Zlătescu, Irina and Oancea, Ioan, *The Legislative and Institutional Framework for the National Minorities of Romania,* Bucureşti: Regia Autonomă Monitorul Oficial, 1994.

Moroianu Zlătescu, Irina and C. Demetrescu, Radu, *Drept instituţional european*, Bucureşti: Editura Olimp, 1999.

Moroianu Zlătescu, Irina, *Constitutional Law in Romania,* The Netherlands: Wolters Kluwer Law and Business, 2013.

Moroianu Zlătescu, Irina, *Codification in the Field of Human Rights,* in *Codification in International Perspective*, ed. Wen-Yeu Wang, Switzerland: Editura Springer International Publishing, 2014.

Moroianu Zlătescu, I. *Human Rights: A Dynamic and Evolving Process*, Bucureşti: Editura Pro Universitaria, 2015.

Moroianu Zlătescu, Irina, *Constitutional Law in Romania*, ed. 2, The Netherlands: Wolters Kluwer, 2017.

Moroianu Zlătescu, Irina and Zlătescu, P. Emanuel, *Enforcement and Effectiveness of Antidiscrimination Law: Romania*, in *Comparative Perspectives on the Enforcement and Effectiveness of Antidiscrimination Law*, ed. Mercat-Bruns, Marie, et al., Switzerland: Springer International Publishing, 2018.

Moroianu Zlătescu, Irina, *Constitutional Law in Romania,* ed. 3, The Netherlands: Wolters Kluwer, 2023.

Moroianu Zlătescu, Irina, *Dreptul International al Drepturilor Omului*, Bucureşti: Editura Universitară, Editura Universul Academic, 2025.

Moroianu Zlătescu, Irina, *Dreptul drepturilor omului*, Bucureşoroi: Editura Universitară, Editura Universul Academic, 2025.

Muraru, Ioan and Constantinescu, Mihai, *Drept parlamentar românesc.* Bucureşti: Editura Actami, 1999.

Muraru, Ioan and Tănăsescu, Elena Simina, *Constituţia României, Comentariu pe articole*, Bucureşti: Editura C.H. Beck, 2008.

Năstase, Adrian, *Drepturile omului: Religie a sfârşitului de secol*, Bucureşti: Editura IRDO, 1992.

Năstase, Adrian, *România Europeană,* Editura MondoMedia, 2007.

Podaru, Ovidiu, *Codul administrativ, Ed. A 5-a/îngrijită şi adnotată de Ovidiu Podaru*, Bucureşti: Editura Hamangiu, 2022.

Popescu-Slăniceanu, Ion, et al., *Drept administrativ,* Galaţi: Editura Universitară Danubius, 2009.

Prodan, David, *Supplex Libellus Valachorum: din istoria formării naţiunii române*, Bucureşti: Editura Enciclopedică, 2013.

Stănciulescu (Alexe), Andreea, *Puterea constituantă. Teoria şi practica puterii constituante*, Bucureşti, Editura C.H. Beck, 2019.

Tilman-Timon, Alexandru. *Les influences etrangéres sur le droit constitutionnel roumain*, Paris: Sirey, 1946.

Toader, Tudorel and Safta, Marieta, *Curs de contencios constituţional*, Bucureşti, Editura Hamangiu, 2017.

Tofan, Dana, *Drept administrativ,* vol. I, Bucureşti: Editura C.H. Beck, 2020.

Vedinas, Verginia, *Codul Administrativ adnotat. Noutati. Examinare comparative.* Note explicative. editia a III-a, revazuta si adaugita, Bucureşti, Editura Universul Juridic, 2021.

Vedinaş, Verginia, *Codul Administrativ comentat. Explicaţii, jurisprudenţă, doctrina* (vols I-II), Bucureşti, Editura Universul Juridic, 2023.

Vida, Ioan, *Curtea Constituţională, justiţia politicului sau politica justiţiei?*, Bucureşti: Editura Monitorul Oficial, 2010.

Zlătescu, Victor Dan and Moroianu Zlătescu, Irina, *Human Rights in Action*, Bucureşti: Editura IRDO, 1993.

Zlătescu, Victor Dan, *Concepts religieux et les droits de l'homme* in *Les droits de l'homme. Dimension spirituelle et action civique*, Bucureşti: Editura IRDO & AIF, 2000.

Selected Bibliography

Index

The numbers here refer to paragraph numbers.

Index

www.ingramcontent.com/pod-product-compliance
Lightning Source LLC
Chambersburg PA
CBHW071344230926
51846CB00002B/445
* 9 7 8 9 4 0 3 5 6 8 7 0 6 *